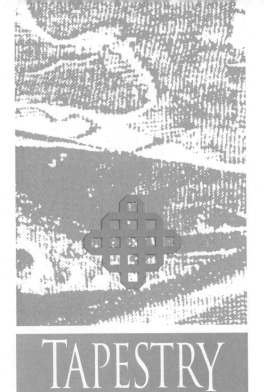

TAPESTRY

WORD
STRAND 2

TAPESTRY

The **Tapestry** program of language materials is based on the concepts presented in *The Tapestry of Language Learning: The Individual in the Communicative Classroom* by Robin C. Scarcella & Rebecca L. Oxford.

Each title in this program focuses on:

Individual learner strategies and instruction

The relatedness of skills

Ongoing self-assessment

Authentic material as input

Theme-based learning linked to task-based instruction

Attention to all aspects of communicative competence

WORD STRAND 2

Meredith Pike-Baky

Laurie Blass

Heinle & Heinle Publishers
An International Thomson
Publishing Company
Boston, Massachusetts, 02116, USA

The publication of *Word Strand 2* was directed by the members of the Heinle & Heinle Global Innovations Publishing Team:

David C. Lee, Editorial Director
John F. McHugh, Market Development Director
Lisa J. McLaughlin, Senior Production Services Coordinator

Also participating in the publication of this program were:
Director of Production: Elizabeth Holthaus
Publisher: Stanley J. Galek
Senior Assistant Editor: Kenneth Mattsson
Production Editor: Maryellen Eschmann Killeen
Manufacturing Coordinator: Mary Beth Hennebury
Full Service Project Manager/Compositor: PC&F, Inc.
Art: Dave Blanchette and PC&F, Inc.
Interior Design: Maureen Lauran
Cover Design: Maureen Lauran
Photo/Video Specialist: Jonathan Stark

Manufactured in the United States of America

ISBN: 0-8384-6074-7

Heinle & Heinle Publishers is an International Thomson Publishing Company.

10 9 8 7 6 5 4 3 2 1

To the memory of Bill Wente,
who really knew how to dance.

PHOTO CREDITS

WELCOME TO TAPESTRY

*E*nter the world of Tapestry! Language learning can be seen as an ever-developing tapestry woven with many threads and colors. The elements of the tapestry are related to different language skills like listening and speaking, reading and writing; the characteristics of the teachers; the desires, needs, and backgrounds of the students; and the general second language development process. When all these elements are working together harmoniously, the result is a colorful, continuously growing tapestry of language competence of which the student and the teacher can be proud.

This volume is part of the Tapestry Program for students of English as a second language (ESL) at levels from beginning to "bridge" (which follows the advanced level and prepares students to enter regular postsecondary programs along with native English speakers). Upper level materials in the Tapestry Program are also appropriate for developmental English courses—especially reading and composition courses. Tapestry levels include:

Beginning   Advanced
Low Intermediate   High Advanced
High Intermediate   Bridge

Because the Tapestry Program provides a unified theoretical and pedagogical foundation for all its components, you can optimally use all the Tapestry student books in a coordinated fashion as an entire curriculum of materials. (They will be published from 1993 to 1996 with further editions likely thereafter.) Alternatively, you can decide to use just certain Tapestry volumes, depending on your specific needs.

Tapestry is primarily designed for ESL students at postsecondary institutions in North America. Some want to learn ESL for academic or career advancement, others for social and personal reasons. Tapestry builds directly on all these motivations. Tapestry stimulates learners to do their best. It enables learners to use English naturally and to develop fluency as well as accuracy.

Tapestry Principles

The following principles underlie the instruction provided in all of the components of the Tapestry Program.

EMPOWERING LEARNERS

Language learners in Tapestry classrooms are active and increasingly responsible for developing their English language skills and related cultural abilities. This self direction leads to better, more rapid learning. Some cultures virtually train their students to be passive in the classroom, but Tapestry weans them from passivity by providing exceptionally high interest materials, colorful and motivating activities, personalized self-reflection tasks, peer tutoring and other forms of cooperative learning, and powerful learning strategies to boost self direction in learning.

The empowerment of learners creates refreshing new roles for teachers, too. The teacher serves as facilitator, co-communicator, diagnostician, guide, and helper. Teachers are set free to be more creative at the same time their students become more autonomous learners.

HELPING STUDENTS IMPROVE THEIR LEARNING STRATEGIES

Learning strategies are the behaviors or steps an individual uses to enhance his or her learning. Examples are taking notes, practicing, finding a conversation partner, analyzing words, using background knowledge, and controlling anxiety. Hundreds of such strategies have been identified. Successful language learners use language learning strategies that are most effective for them given their particular learning style, and they put them together smoothly to fit the needs of a given language task. On the other hand, the learning strategies of less successful learners are a desperate grab-bag of ill-matched techniques.

All learners need to know a wide range of learning strategies. All learners need systematic practice in choosing and applying strategies that are relevant for various learning needs. Tapestry is one of the only ESL programs that overtly weaves a comprehensive set of learning strategies into language activities in all its volumes. These learning strategies are arranged in eight broad categories throughout the Tapestry books:

Forming Concepts
Personalizing
Remembering New Material
Managing Your Learning
Understanding and Using Emotions
Overcoming Limitations
Testing Hypotheses
Learning with Others

The most useful strategies are sometimes repeated and flagged with a note, "It Works! Learning Strategy . . ." to remind students to use a learning strategy they have already encountered. This recycling reinforces the value of learning strategies and provides greater practice.

RECOGNIZING AND HANDLING LEARNING STYLES EFFECTIVELY

Learners have different learning styles (for instance, visual, auditory, hands-on; reflective, impulsive; analytic, global; extroverted, introverted; closure-oriented, open). Particularly in an ESL setting, where students come from vastly different cultural backgrounds, learning styles differences abound and can cause "style conflicts."

Unlike most language instruction materials, Tapestry provides exciting activities specifically tailored to the needs of students with a large range of learning styles. You can use any Tapestry volume with the confidence that the activities and materials are intentionally geared for many different styles. Insights from the latest educational and psychological research undergird this style-nourishing variety.

OFFERING AUTHENTIC, MEANINGFUL COMMUNICATION

Students need to encounter language that provides authentic, meaningful communication. They must be involved in real-life communication tasks that cause them to *want* and *need* to read, write, speak, and listen to English. Moreover, the tasks—to be most effective—must be arranged around themes relevant to learners.

Themes like family relationships, survival in the educational system, personal health, friendships in a new country, political changes, and protection of the environment are all valuable to ESL learners. Tapestry focuses on topics like these. In every Tapestry volume, you will see specific content drawn from very broad areas such as home life, science and technology, business, humanities, social sciences, global issues, and multiculturalism. All the themes are real and important, and they are fashioned into language tasks that students enjoy.

At the advanced level, Tapestry also includes special books each focused on a single broad theme. For instance, there are two books on business English, two on English for science and technology, and two on academic communication and study skills.

UNDERSTANDING AND VALUING DIFFERENT CULTURES

Many ESL books and programs focus completely on the "new" culture, that is, the culture which the students are entering. The implicit message is that ESL students should just learn about this target culture, and there is no need to understand their own culture better or to find out about the cultures of their international classmates. To some ESL students, this makes them feel their own culture is not valued in the new country.

Tapestry is designed to provide a clear and understandable entry into North American culture. Nevertheless, the Tapestry Program values *all* the cultures found in the ESL classroom. Tapestry students have constant opportunities to become "culturally fluent" in North American culture while they are learning English, but they also have the chance to think about the cultures of their classmates and even understand their home culture from different perspectives.

INTEGRATING THE LANGUAGE SKILLS

Communication in a language is not restricted to one skill or another. ESL students are typically expected to learn (to a greater or lesser degree) all four language skills: reading, writing, speaking, and listening. They are also expected to develop strong grammatical competence, as well as becoming socioculturally sensitive and knowing what to do when they encounter a "language barrier."

Research shows that multi-skill learning is more effective than isolated-skill learning, because related activities in several skills provide reinforcement and refresh the learner's memory. Therefore, Tapestry integrates all the skills. A given Tapestry volume might highlight one skill, such as reading, but all other skills are also included to support and strengthen overall language development.

However, many intensive ESL programs are divided into classes labeled according to one skill (Reading Comprehension Class) or at most two skills (Listening/Speaking Class or Oral Communication Class). The volumes in the Tapestry Program can easily be used to fit this traditional format, because each volume clearly identifies its highlighted or central skill(s).

Grammar is interwoven into all Tapestry volumes. However, there is also a separate reference book for students, *The Tapestry Grammar,* and a Grammar Strand composed of grammar "work-out" books at each of the levels in the Tapestry Program.

Other Features of the Tapestry Program

PILOT SITES

It is not enough to provide volumes full of appealing tasks and beautiful pictures. Users deserve to know that the materials have been pilot-tested. In many ESL series, pilot testing takes place at only a few sites or even just in the classroom of the author. In contrast, Heinle & Heinle Publishers have developed a network of Tapestry Pilot Test Sites throughout North America. At this time, there are approximately 40 such sites, although the number grows weekly. These sites try out the materials and provide suggestions for revisions. They are all actively engaged in making Tapestry the best program possible.

AN OVERALL GUIDEBOOK

To offer coherence to the entire Tapestry Program and especially to offer support for teachers who want to understand the principles and practice of Tapestry, we have written a book entitled, *The Tapestry of Language Learning. The Individual in the Communicative Classroom* (Scarcella and Oxford, published in 1992 by Heinle & Heinle).

A Last Word

We are pleased to welcome you to Tapestry! We use the Tapestry principles every day, and we hope these principles—and all the books in the Tapestry Program—provide you the same strength, confidence, and joy that they give us. We look forward to comments from both teachers and students who use any part of the Tapestry Program.

Rebecca L. Oxford
University of Alabama
Tuscaloosa, Alabama

Robin C. Scarcella
University of California at Irvine
Irvine, California

PREFACE

Word Strand 2 is a vocabulary program designed to address the needs of students in high-beginning or low-intermediate English as a Second Language classes. It is appropriate for adult and intensive programs at secondary through university levels. *Word Strand 2* can serve as the core text for a vocabulary class or as a supplemental text for a reading, fluency, or all-skills course. Instructors can choose chapters in any order according to the interests of the students, the calendar, or current issues and topics, or move through the chapters sequentially and take advantage of recycling activities in each.

We feel strongly that any vocabulary-building program at the high-beginning to low-intermediate level works best if:

- context is the departure point for learning a *set* of words that respond to a particular theme, task, setting, or situation
- the context is real and dynamic
- the context offers opportunities for students to connect text material to their immediate lives
- students are able to *interact* with the text by labeling word lists, writing captions for photos, and adding some of their own relevant material
- students see the same words in similar and different contexts
- students work in various configurations (individually, in pairs, triads, small groups, and teams) to complete tasks
- students have regular opportunities to reflect on their learning and assess their progress
- the content is fresh and lively, so it is fun to study and fun to teach

Word Strand 2 radiates from five umbrella concepts that suggest useful themes and meaningful contexts for high-beginning students of English as a Second Language. These are Places, People, Food, Fun, and Tools. In turn, each theme generates two chapters that provide opportunities for students to learn new words and review and recycle old words. For example, Chapter 5 is *Food: What Would You Like to Eat?* In this chapter, students talk about food preferences. Chapter 6 is *Food: What's in It?* Here, students talk about what goes into favorite and familiar foods. In this way, students increase their ability to communicate about related topics.

How *Word Strand 2* Is Organized

A typical *Word Strand* 2 chapter has the following sequence:

PART 1: WORDS IN CONTEXT

This section begins by presenting the chapter's key vocabulary and concepts through art and authentic reading passages accompanied by brainstorming and analysis activities. These activities build confidence by requiring students to draw upon prior knowledge as they explore new material. The section winds up with the Word Bank, a listing of all the new words in the chapter. Each Word Bank is followed by a series of questions that elicits useful facts about the items—rules associated with spelling, pronunciation, semantics, and syntax. This activity not only helps students learn the meaning but the form and use of new words.

PART 2: WORD EXTENSIONS

Word Extensions include activities that help students generate additional lexical items based on those presented in Part I. These activities teach students how to extend their vocabularies on their own by generating synonyms, antonyms, and creating new forms through the use of affixes. When appropriate, this section also includes activities that present and practice rules of structure and usage particular to some of the vocabulary items.

PART 3: USING WORDS

This section lets students use the vocabulary presented in the chapter in a variety of creative and authentic speaking and writing activities. These activities:

- promote critical thinking skills
- help students personalize concepts
- allow students to synthesize material from the current and previous chapters and put it to use in new, real-life situations

The section also includes one or more word games. These games direct the students to work in teams in order to reinforce new vocabulary.

PART 4: ASSESSMENT

The Assessment section has two components. The first part allows students to review and test themselves on chapter material. The second part is student-centered: it enables students to assess their learning in terms of their own needs, and extend the learning experience by setting personal goals. Students can look forward to this opportunity in every chapter.

Acknowledgments

We gratefully acknowledge the support and inspiration of Dave Lee, Ken Mattsson, Rebecca Oxford, and Robin Scarcella. In addition, we would like to thank the following reviewers, whose comments were invaluable in the shaping of this book:

Susana Christie, San Diego State University;

Debra Dean, University of Akron;

John Fitzer, State University of New York at Buffalo;

Pamela Flash, University of Minnesota;

Keith Folse, University of Southern Florida;

Kelly Franklin, Maryville College;

Guillermo Perez, Miami-Dade Community College;

Graciela Helguero, Florida Language Center; and

Margene Petersen, ELS Philadelphia.

To the Student

Welcome to *Word Strand 2*! With help from this book, your classmates, and your teacher, you will develop your vocabulary, build your confidence, and increase your fluency in English. Before you begin, we would like to give you a few tips:

- Start a Word Journal. A Word Journal is a notebook just for words. In it, write down each new word you learn. Give each group of new words a title. For example, the first group of new words you will see in Chapter 1 is Places. Use word group titles from the book or think of your own. In each word group, organize the new words into lists that will help you. You might choose to list words according to parts of speech: Nouns, Verbs, Adjectives, etc. Or you might group words according to what you have trouble with: Words That Are Hard to Spell, Words That Are Hard to Remember, etc.
- Practice using your new words often. Try them out when you talk to your friends and classmates. Review your Word Journal.
- When a native speaker uses a new word you've never heard before, ask him or her what it means. Then write it in your Word Journal.

Finally, we would like to know how this book works for you and what words you add to it. Send us a letter c/o Heinle & Heinle, 20 Park Plaza, Boston, MA. 02116. You can also contact us by e-mail at tapestry@heinle.com.

Meredith Pike-Baky and Laurie Blass

CONTENTS

4   People: How Do You Learn Best?   37

5   Food: What Would You Like to Eat?   51

6   Food: What's in It?   61

10 Tools: How Do You Get Information? 105

Places: What's in Your Community?

PLACES: WHAT'S IN YOUR COMMUNITY?

What are the important places in any community you visit? In this chapter you will study a community map and locate important places. You will also learn about the people who work in these places.

PART 1: WORDS IN CONTEXT

Take a Look

Look at the following photos of community places. With a partner, write the name for each place under each photo. If you're not sure, make a guess.

1. _____

2. _____

4. _____

3. _____

5. _____

6. _____

7. _____

8. _____

Threads

A *town* is a community of closely clustered dwellings and other buildings in which people live and work.

Now answer these questions:

1. Where do people go when they are sick?
2. Is there a place where people can borrow books?
3. Where can you play basketball?
4. Which places are busy on weekends? Which places are more active during the week?
5. At which places would you find more children than adults? Where would you find more adults than children?
6. Are there any places listed that you don't have in your community? Which ones?
7. What places would you like to add? Draw three more places above numbers 6, 7, and 8. Write their names, then share your answers with your classmates. Explain why you added these places and if you use them.

Threads

A typical neighborhood park has these facilities: ballfield, basketball court, community building, horseshoe pits, jogging trails, a picnic area, a playground and restrooms.

Read About It

Study the following community map.

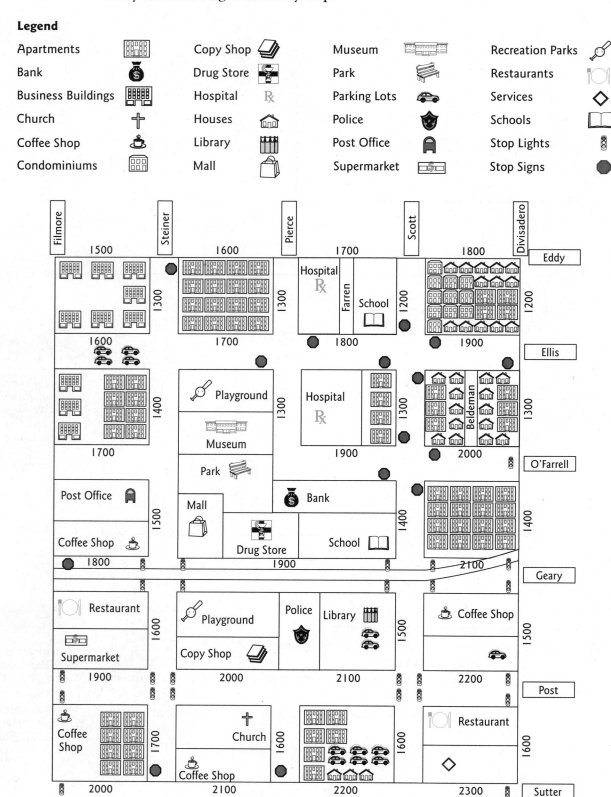

Legend

Apartments		Copy Shop		Museum		Recreation Parks	
Bank		Drug Store		Park		Restaurants	
Business Buildings		Hospital	Rx	Parking Lots		Services	
Church		Houses		Police		Schools	
Coffee Shop		Library		Post Office		Stop Lights	
Condominiums		Mall		Supermarket		Stop Signs	

Check Your Understanding

Remembering New Material: Putting new words into categories
helps you remember them better.

1. Refer to your community map. Write the names of places in the following
categories. You may write a place in more than one category and you can add
places of your own.

Places Where You Buy Things

_____

_____

_____

Places Where You Visit People

_____

_____

_____

Places Where You Look at Things

_____

_____

_____

Places Where You Borrow Things

_____

_____

_____

Places Where You Go for Help

_____

_____

_____

Places Where You _____

_____

_____

_____

Threads

The word *hospital* comes
from the Latin word
hospitium, which means
a *house* or *institution
for guests.*

Forming New Concepts: Looking for relationships between places
and activities increases your understanding of both.

2. Draw a line from the name of the place to the activity describing what people
can do there.

PLACES	WHAT YOU DO THERE
school	buy groceries
hospital	watch a movie
playground	eat a meal
supermarket	look at paintings
post office	have a picnic
shopping mall	visit a sick patient
library	learn new words
restaurant	buy stamps
museum	buy a shirt
theatre	read a magazine

3. Who works in these places? Match the name of each place in a community with the people who work there.

PLACES	PEOPLE WHO WORK THERE
school	waitress
hospital	clerk
playground	doctor
supermarket	cashier
post office	teacher
shopping mall	recreation supervisor
library	guide
restaurant	store manager
museum	librarian
theatre	usher

Word Bank

PLACES, PEOPLE, THINGS

Here are the new words for this chapter. Add them to your Word Journal.

PLACES	PEOPLE	THINGS
apartment	cashier	groceries
basketball court	clerk	letter
hospital	customer	location
library	doctor	movie
museum	guide	meal
neighborhood	librarian	paintings
playground	recreation supervisor	picnic
post office	store manager	patient
restaurant	teacher	words
school	usher	stamps
shopping mall	waitress	shirt
supermarket		magazine
tennis court		
theatre		
park		

Questions

❶ Which two words from the Word Bank can be two parts of speech?

HINT   One word is both a noun and an adjective, and another is both a noun and a verb.

❷ Which word from the Word Bank is spelled differently in British and American English?

❸ *Waitress* refers to a female; what is the male form of this word?

❹ True or false: These words have the same stress and intonation: *shopping mall, magazine, hospital*.

Answers

❹ **True. The first syllable is stressed.**

❸ **Waiter**

❷ *Theatre* is British English and *theater* is American English. They have the same pronunciation.

❶ *Patient* is a noun and an adjective; *stamp* is a noun and a verb.

Prepositions

It is useful to review prepositions when talking or writing about places. Study these expressions which describe location. Each box contains words or expressions with the same meaning.

on top of above over on	close to near by adjacent to	far away from far from
in back of behind	under below underneath beneath	between in between
next to beside	in front of	in inside

1. Use at least one expression from each box to describe the location of some places in the community from the map in Part 1.

   EXAMPLE   *Beideman Street is **between** two blocks of houses and apartments.*

2. Now use at least one expression from each box to describe the location of places in your community.

LEARNING STRATEGY

Overcoming Limitations: Learning how to use new words increases your fluency.

Adjectives

Extend your ability to talk about places by using adjectives that describe them. Study this list of adjectives and their meanings.

ADJECTIVES	MEANINGS
crowded	There are lots of people (or lots of pieces of furniture) there.
new	It was built recently.
expensive	It costs lots of money to buy things there.
modern	It is not old-fashioned.
well-organized	It is orderly.
well-equipped	It has the necessary equipment.
spacious	There is lots of space here.
popular	Many people like this place.

1. Which adjectives would you use to describe these places?

   a park with lots of fields _____

   a school with many computers _____

   a restaurant that is always full _____

   a playground with swings, climbing structures, basketball, tennis courts, and benches _____

   a supermarket where every aisle is clearly labelled _____

   a museum designed by a young architect with lots of windows and skylights

   _____

2. Practice these adjectives by describing places in your community. With a partner, take turns asking and answering questions like these:

   EXAMPLES   *Where is a place in the community that is **modern**?*

   *The engineering building on campus is **modern**. It has green marble on the outside walls and there are trees everywhere.*

3. Add new words from this section to your Word Journal.

PART 3: USING WORDS

Use Words Creatively

1. In small groups, talk about your favorite places in the community. Use lots of "showing language"—the prepositions and adjectives you studied on pages 7-8—in your descriptions so that your classmates can "see" these places by listening to your words.

Threads

The Public Library at São Paulo has a large auditorium, as well as soundproof rooms for music and for research.

Threads

The word *museu* comes from the Greek word *mouseion*, meaning *temple of the muses*, or *a place to study.*

Personalizing Your Learning: Connecting familiar places to new words will help you use and remember them.

2. Visit a place in your community where you can sit and observe quietly. Take notes on what you see, hear, and feel. Use this chart to record your impressions then share it with your classmates.

Place: _____

WHAT YOU SEE	WHAT YOU HEAR	HOW YOU FEEL

3. Write a paragraph about your favorite place. Add a map, photo, or illustration if possible.

Managing Your Learning: Presenting what you've learned to classmates encourages you to reflect on your learning.

Word Game

JEOPARDY

This is a version of a popular television game. In this game, players think of correct *questions* to go with answers. Divide into two teams. Take turns giving answers. Each correct question wins a point. There can be more than one correct question for each answer. The team with the most points at the end of the game wins.

> ***EXAMPLE*** Answer: Doctors and nurses work here.
> Question: What is a hospital?

    Answers

a. You can find one at a playground.
b. I buy stamps there.
c. I live in one.
d. It is usually crowded at dinnertime.
e. Students spend their days here.

Now continue with your own answers.

PART 4: ASSESSMENT

Review

Review the new words from this chapter by circling the one word that relates in meaning to the word in the left column. Make sure you can explain how the word you circled relates to the word on the left.

1. **library**	hospital	books	meal
2. **waitress**	patient	location	restaurant
3. **on top of**	above	beneath	in back of
4. **groceries**	restaurant	supermarket	guide
5. **museum**	usher	doctor	guide
6. **basketball court**	playground	museum	library
7. **apartment**	doctor	theater	house
8. **teacher**	post office	school	theater
9. **cashier**	supermarket	guide	doctor
10. **borrow**	buy	post office	library

Test Yourself

The following is a section from a tour book that was written for young people who go abroad to study. Use words from this chapter to fill in the blanks.

supermarket	shopping mall	apartment	restaurant	school
post office	community	hospital	library	museum

As a visitor to a new place, one of the first things you should do is learn the locations of important places in the _____ . After moving
₁
into your house or _____ , you should get to know where
₂
all the important locations are. The most important places, of course, will depend on how you spend your time. If you are a student, you will want to find the _____ immediately. You will also want to locate
₃
the cafeteria or a _____ where you can eat cheaply. If you
₄
can use a kitchen, you'll want to look for a _____ to
₅
buy food.

Of secondary importance are the places you'll visit regularly, but not every day. You'll want to make sure you know how to get to the _____ to buy stamps and mail letters and postcards.
₆
You'll also want to know the location of the _____ in
₇
case you get sick and need to see a doctor. You will probably want to know where the _____ is for late-night studying and where the
₈
closest _____ is to buy clothes and souvenirs.
₉

Finally, you'll want to know where you can go to have fun. You may want to go to the movies on the weekends, so you'll want to learn the location of the closest theater. And maybe you'll want to visit a _____
₁₀
nearby to learn something about the local history. Learning the important places in your new neighborhood is one of the best ways to adjust to a new place.

Look Back

What did you learn about places in a community from this chapter?

_____

_____

_____

_____

Look Ahead

What else do you want to learn about community places? How do you plan to do it?

_____

_____

_____

_____

_____

Places: How Do You Get There?

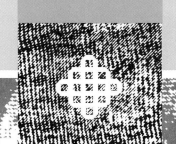

There are many different ways to travel long distances. In this chapter, you're going to look at different kinds of transportation.

PART 1: WORDS IN CONTEXT

Take a Look

Take a look at these photos. In small groups, name the kind of transportation in each one. Also, talk about what you like or dislike about each kind of transportation.

1. _____

2. _____

3. _____

4. _____

Now, match the following expressions with the photos. There may be more than one expression for some photos. Write the number of the photo(s) in the blank after each expression.

travel by car _____   travel by boat _____

travel by bus _____   travel by train _____

travel by rail _____   travel by ship _____

travel by sea _____   travel by air _____

travel by land _____

Threads

The Greyhound Bus Company was founded in Minnesota in 1916 by Carl Eric Wickman, a Swedish miner-turned-car salesman.

The Ethnic Almanac

Read About It

Read these travel ads from the newspaper:

STUDENT TRAVEL INC.
Cheap airline tickets to wherever you want to go!

INTERNATIONAL

DOMESTIC

	one way/round trip		one way/round trip
		Paris	$250/$500
Los Angeles	$175/$350	Hong Kong	$400/$800
San Francisco	$200/$400	Mexico City	$175/$350
New York	$150/$300		

E-Z Rent-a-Car
Cars as low as $18.50 per day, plus unlimited mileage!
Special weekend rates!
(From Friday 5:00 PM to Sunday 5:00 PM)
Call 800-555-3420
Get out of town this weekend!

Discount Cruises to Mexico!!
Fares from $599!!
Exotic Destinations!!
Depart: 3/12   Return: 4/1
Itinerary:
• Los Angeles
• Puerto Vallarta
• Ixtapa
• Acapulco
• Mazatlan
• Cabo San Lucas
• Los Angeles

GLOBAL TRAVEL
59970 Pico Blvd.
Los Angeles

Call 800-555-1695 today!!

TRAVEL SUPERMARKET
The best in discount travel!
• Discount railpasses for
   England
   Europe
   Japan
• 40% off business class air tickets on many airlines
• Charter flights!
   Domestic and international destinations
Call 1-800-555-9398
for our incredibly low fares!!!

LEARNING STRATEGY

Remembering New Material: Learning new words in realistic contexts helps you remember them better.

Check Your Understanding

Work with a partner and answer these questions about the ads:

1. How many kinds of transportation do you see in these ads? What are they?
2. Give an example of a domestic destination in the ads.
3. Give an example of an international destination in the ads.
4. Which companies sell cheap international airline tickets?
5. Which company sells railpasses?
6. What should you ask for at E-Z Rent-a-Car if you want a car from Friday to Sunday?
7. What do you think "unlimited mileage" means at a car rental company?
8. If you take Global Travel's cruise to Mexico, how many places in Mexico do you visit?

Threads

The U.S. highway system stretches over 3.8 million miles.

The Ethnic Almanac

Word Bank

Here are the new words for this chapter. Add them to your Word Journal.

GETTING THERE

charter	discount	flight		car
depart	cheap	unlimited		ship
destination	one way	fare		sea
cruise	travel	international		air
class (first,	rate	return	travel by	land
business,	mileage	ticket		boat
coach)	domestic	rent (a car)		bus
ad	itinerary	exotic		train
round trip	railpass			rail

LEARNING STRATEGY

Forming Concepts: Analyzing new words helps you understand them more fully.

Questions

❶ Which words in the Word Bank are adjectives? Nouns? Verbs? Group the words in the list by part of speech. Put a check (✓) next to words that have more than one part of speech when you're talking about travel.

❷ How do you stress the following words: *itinerary, domestic, destination, international*?

❸ Which of the following words rhymes with *cruise*?

loose   *lice*   *lose*

❹ Do any expressions in the "travel by" list mean about the same thing? What are they?

❺ What's the difference between a *fare* and a *rate*?

Answers

❶ Adjectives: *charter* ✓ *round trip, domestic, international, cheap, one way*
Nouns: *ticket* ✓ *travel* ✓ *flight, mileage, fare, rate, discount* ✓ *destination, itinerary, cruise* ✓ *railpass, class*
Verbs: *ticket* ✓ *travel* ✓ *rent, discount* ✓ *cruise* ✓ *depart, return,* all the
"travel by" expressions, *charter* ✓

❷ *iTINerary, doMEstic, destiNAtion, interNAtional*

❸ *Lose* rhymes with *cruise*.

❹ Yes. *Travel by sea, boat, ship* mean about the same thing.
Travel by train, rail mean about the same thing.

❺ We only use *fare* when we talk about travel; we use *rate* in many contexts, for example, rate of exchange (money).

PART 2: WORD EXTENSIONS

Synonyms

LEARNING STRATEGY

Overcoming Limitations: Guessing synonyms of words you already know helps you become more confident.

Knowing synonyms for new words helps you extend your vocabulary and understand meanings better. You've seen the words listed on the left in the ads on page 15. Now see if you can match each of these with the word or expression that means about the same thing on the right:

cheap	price
depart	within the country
return	to reserve for a group
itinerary	outside the country
domestic	inexpensive
international	a travel plan
fare	come back
charter (verb)	leave

Structure: Gerund Subjects

You can use many of the verbs in the Word Bank as nouns by adding -*ing*. You can use them as subjects of sentences. Doing this adds variety to your language.

> **EXAMPLE** *Traveling* by train is cheaper than *traveling* by air.
>
> *Traveling* comes from the verb *to travel*—just add -*ing*.

If the verb ends with a vowel followed by a consonant and has only one syllable, you double the final consonant before you add -*ing*.

> **EXAMPLE** *to get* —> *Getting* to the airport on time is important.

If the verb ends in -*e*, drop the -*e*, then add -*ing*.

> **EXAMPLE** *cruise* —> *Cruising* the Caribbean is my favorite kind of vacation.

Threads

The first American airplane was a flown by its inventors, the Wright Brothers, December 17, 1903, on a sandy beach near Kitty Hawk, North Carolina.

The People's Almanac

1. Complete these sentences with the gerund (-*ing*) form of the verb from the following list.

| travel by sea | cruise | travel by air | travel by land |
| rent | travel by train | travel by car | |

   (You may not use all of them.)

   a. _____ is too expensive for me.

   b. _____ always makes me sick.

   c. _____ takes too long.

   d. _____ is cheaper than _____ .

   e. _____ is more fun than _____ .

2. Work in small groups. Use gerund subjects to talk about the kind of transportation you like or dislike. Give reasons.

   > **EXAMPLE** Traveling by train is fun because I can see where I'm going.

PART 3: USING WORDS

Use Words Creatively

1. In small groups, talk about what you like and dislike about different kinds of travel: renting a car, going on a charter flight, taking the bus or train for long distances, etc. Talk about:

   • cost
   • comfort
   • the time it takes
   • whether one way is easier to meet new people
   • pollution
   • other advantages and disadvantages

2. With a partner, plan a trip. Leave from one place, and go to two other places before you return home. Talk about the kinds of transportation you will use, and why you will use them.

3. Write about the kind of transportation you would choose for one of the following trips:
   - a weekend trip to a friend who lives 400 miles away
   - a weekend visit with a friend who lives 50 miles away
   - going home to visit your family for the summer
   - going on a vacation in a foreign country
   - going on a vacation in a country that is across an ocean
   - visiting an exotic place

Word Game

WORD SEARCH

Find and circle the following words from the Word Bank in the Word Search grid. They can be vertical ↕, horizontal ↔, on a diagonal ↘, or backwards ←.

charter	destination	itinerary	cruise
domestic	depart	discount	

Word Search

W	E	E	A	D	E	S	T	N	E	S	T
S	G	H	H	E	I	Y	U	I	O	H	E
Y	Y	B	O	S	U	S	I	A	J	L	D
E	R	A	O	T	I	O	C	D	O	P	O
P	A	R	T	I	O	N	T	O	C	W	M
P	R	E	S	N	Q	U	D	C	U	T	E
D	E	C	H	A	R	T	E	R	I	N	S
I	N	O	A	T	I	O	P	U	A	R	T
S	I	T	O	I	N	P	A	I	B	S	I
O	T	I	R	O	I	O	R	S	T	A	C
I	I	O	T	N	R	Y	T	E	A	R	T

Recycle

Do the following activity in small groups. Combine words from this chapter with words from Chapter 1.

Some friends are coming from far away to visit your town. First, tell them how to get there. Then tell them about places in your community to visit and what kind of transportation they can take to get around town.

Optional: Write your answer to the Recycle activity.

PART 4: ASSESSMENT

Review

Review words from this chapter by taking the following quiz. Work with a partner, and see how quickly you can fill in the blanks with the correct words.

1. A plan for a trip is a(n) _____.
   a. destination
   b. railpass
   c. itinerary
2. If you aren't coming back from a trip, you buy a(n) _____ ticket.
   a. discount
   b. one way
   c. round trip
3. A destination outside of the country is _____.
   a. domestic
   b. first class
   c. international
4. A train ticket that lets you go many places for one fare is a(n) _____.
   a. railpass
   b. cruise
   c. itinerary
5. Another way to say *travel by rail* is _____.
   a. travel by sea
   b. travel by air
   c. travel by train
6. A low-cost fare is a _____ fare.
   a. discount
   b. cheap
   c. both a and b
7. When a group reserves a plane for a low fare, it's a _____ flight.
   a. round trip
   b. domestic
   c. charter
8. A first class ticket is more expensive than a _____ ticket.
   a. round trip
   b. coach
   c. international

9. When you go on a cruise, you travel by _____ .
   a. sea
   b. land
   c. air

10. When you rent a car, you sometimes have to pay for the _____ .
    a. ad
    b. return
    c. mileage

Test Yourself

LEARNING STRATEGY

Managing Your Learning: Testing yourself helps you become a more independent learner.

Complete this travel ad using these words from the Word Bank. Some answers are correct in more than one space but use each word only once.

first	fares	discount	charter
international	destinations	round trip	cruises
mileage	prices		

The Travel Shop

We've got the lowest _____ in town!
              1

Low cost travel to many _____ !
                2

Domestic and _____ !
          3

• _____ tickets to Europe and Asia
     4

	One Way	_____
		5
Paris	$350	$700
London	$320	$640
Tokyo	$400	$800
Singapore	$450	$900

• 40% off _____ and business class air tickets on many airlines.
       6

• Discount _____ to Mexico!
       7

Travel to these exotic destinations by sea!

    Puerto Vallarta   Mazatlan   Acapulco

• _____ flights for groups of 30 or more
      8

• Low cost car rentals. Weekend rates. Unlimited _____ .
                9

Call 1-800-555-4967 for our incredibly low _____ !!!
                      10

Look Back

What did you learn about words that describe different kinds of transportation?

_____

_____

_____

_____

_____

Threads

So far as my experience goes, travelers generally exaggerate the difficulties of the way.

H.D. Thoreau, _A Week on the Concord and Merrimac Rivers: Tuesday_

Look Ahead

What else do you want to learn about different kinds of transportation? How do you plan to do this?

_____

_____

_____

_____

_____

People: Who Are These Famous Women?

PEOPLE: WHO ARE THESE FAMOUS WOMEN?

In the past, history books have contained much about famous men. But what about famous women? In this chapter you will identify and describe some famous international women.

PART 1: WORDS IN CONTEXT

Take a Look

Look at the following photos of famous international women from the twentieth century. Work with a partner. Try to guess who they were, where they came from, and what they did. Write this information below each photo.

1. _____
   _____
   _____
   _____

2. _____
   _____
   _____
   _____

3. _____
   _____
   _____

4. _____

_____

_____

5. _____

_____

_____

6. _____

_____

_____

7. _____

_____

_____

8. _____

_____

_____

Now check your information with another pair of students. Together, think of two more women to add to this list.

LEARNING STRATEGY

Forming Concepts: Adding your own information will make new material more meaningful.

Read About It.

Read the following fact chart.

FAMOUS TWENTIETH CENTURY WOMEN

NAME	BIRTH AND BACKGROUND	ACTIVITIES AND ACCOMPLISHMENTS
Rosa Parks	• born in 1913 in Tuskegee, Alabama	• was a central figure in the U.S. civil rights movement • started the bus boycott by refusing to give up seat
Rigoberta Menchu	• born in 1959 in Guatemala • went into exile in Mexico in 1981 after family was killed	• won the Nobel Peace Prize in 1992 • spokesperson for indigenous people throughout the Americas • wrote *I, Rigoberta Menchu*
Ella Fitzgerald	• born in 1918 in Newport News, Virginia	• singer who had strong influence on several generations of popular music singers • sang with Duke Ellington and Count Basie, and was a soloist with more than 40 symphony orchestras
Golda Meir	• born in 1898 in Kiev, Russia • family emigrated to Wisconsin in 1906 • moved to Palestine in 1921 • died in 1978	• Prime Minister of Israel from 1969–1974 • became first female foreign minister of Israel in 1956 • helped shape policies of Israel
Eleanor Roosevelt	• born in 1884 in New York City • niece of President Theodore Roosevelt • raised by grandmother after early death of parents • died in 1962	• although shy, became active in politics when husband got polio in 1921 • spoke out for social causes when husband was president • had radio program, wrote a newspaper column, defended civil rights for blacks and women
Mother Teresa	• born in 1910 in Albania • became a Catholic nun at 18 and went to India to teach school • retired in 1990	• dedicated to helping the poor, she is known for her work in Calcutta, India • established an orphanage, hospital, and religious community • won the Nobel Peace Prize in 1979
Amelia Earhart	• born in 1898 in Atchison, Kansas • died in 1937 during attempt to complete flight around the world	• first woman pilot to cross Atlantic Ocean alone • first woman pilot to fly from Honolulu to the United States • first woman pilot to fly across the United States in both directions
Jackie Joyner Kersee	• born in 1962 in East St. Louis, Ill. • comes from a family of American track and field stars	• set U.S. record for long-jump in 1987 • won 100 meter hurdles in 1994 Pan African Games • first woman selected Athlete of the Year by *Sporting News*
Indira Gandhi	• born in 1917 • only child of Jawaharlal Nehru, India's first Prime Minister • assassinated in 1984	• became India's first female Prime Minister in 1966 • became Minister of Information in 1964 • became president of Indian National Congress in 1959
Maya Angelou	• born in 1928 in St. Louis, Mo. • grew up in segregated Arkansas	• poet for Bill Clinton's inauguration in 1993 and for United Nations' 50th Anniversary in 1995 • wrote *I Know Why the Caged Bird Sings* (1970) and other autobiographical accounts of her life as well as collections of poetry and fiction • has written plays, screenplays, and has composed songs and musical scores
Benazir Bhutto	• born in 1953 in Pakistan • daughter of Zulfikar Ali Bhutto who formed Pakistan People's Party and was head of government 1971–1977	• first woman to head modern Moslem state as Pakistan's Prime Minister • in exile 1984–1986 • under arrest 1981–1984

Check Your Understanding

Try to answer these questions alone, and then check your answers with a partner.

1. Which women are still alive? How old are these women today?

   _____

2. Which women are/were active in politics?

   _____

3. Which women did things that no women had done before?

   _____

4. Which women came from famous families?

   _____

5. Which women are/were singers?

   _____

6. Which women were born in the United States?

   _____

7. Which women were courageous?

   _____

8. Which women had backgrounds or early years that helped them become great?

   _____

LEARNING STRATEGY

Overcoming Limitations: Appying new words in different contexts will help you understand and use the new words quickly.

9. Make a list of 10 famous twentieth-century men. Try to think of men who have qualities you've already discussed. Share your list with your class.
10. Match adjectives on the left with the names of women on the right. Explain your answers to a partner.

talented	Rosa Parks
	Rigoberta Menchu
courageous	Ella Fitzgerald
	Golda Meir
athletic	Eleanor Roosevelt
	Mother Theresa
intelligent	Amelia Earhart
	Jacki Joyner-Kersee
dedicated	Indira Gandhi
	Maya Angelou

LEARNING STRATEGY

Remembering New Material: Keeping a Word Journal helps you learn new words and remember old words.

Word Bank

Here are the new words presented in this chapter. Answer the questions after each group of words then add new words to your Word Journal.

FAMOUS PEOPLE

athletic	intelligent
central	popular
courageous	skillful
dedicated	smart
determined	spokesperson
heroic	strong
innovative	talented

Questions

1. These words are all the same part of speech. Are they nouns, verbs, adjectives or adverbs?
2. *To innovate* and *to dedicate* are verbs related to two adjectives from the list. What do you think the verbs mean?
3. Where is the stress in these words: *innovative, courageous, dedicated?*
4. *Strong* can refer to physical strength, but there are other kinds of strength. Give an example of another type of strength.
5. Which of the adjectives from the list would you use to describe yourself?

Answers

5. Answers will vary. Is there a student who claims to be all of these?
4. There is *political* strength (when Indira Gandhi was first elected Prime Minister of India), *emotional* strength (when Eleanor Roosevelt learned that her husband had polio, she overcame shyness and became politically active), and *psychological* strength (which Mother Teresa demonstrated as she helped the poorest of the poor in Calcutta).
3. The stress is on these syllables: INNovative, couRAgeous, DEdicated.
2. *To innovate* means to begin or do something for the first time; *to dedicate* means to offer something to someone.
1. All of the words are adjectives.

WHAT FAMOUS PEOPLE DO

boycott	heal
compete	improve people's lives
compose	initiate
create	inspire
defend	lead
educate	perform
emigrate	refuse
establish	retire
explore	set a record for
face difficulties	shape policies
fight	speak out for
go into exile	struggle
have an influence on	win a prize
have dreams	write

Questions

1. These words and phrases are all the same part of speech. Are they nouns, verbs, adjectives or adverbs?
2. The noun forms of *compete, educate, establish, explore, initiate,* and *perform* end in *-tion, -ment,* or *-ance,* Try to make these verbs nouns by guessing the correct suffix.
3. Which word is the same for both verb and noun forms?
4. Which word rhymes with *heal: real, well,* or *hail?*
5. Which two words from the list rhyme?
6. What are some different accomplishments a person can set a record for?
7. Which can you NOT have an influence on: people, generations, or weather?
8. What prize would you like to win?

Answers

1. These are verbs or verb phrases.
2. The noun forms are *competition, education, establishment, exploration, initiation,* and *performance.*
3. *Fight* is both noun and verb.
4. *Real* rhymes with *heal.*
5. *Write* and *fight* rhyme.
6. You can *set a record* for being the first, youngest, oldest, fastest person to do anything. You can *set a record* for being the first person from your country to do something.
7. You cannot *have an influence on* the weather.
8. Answers will vary. Some possibilities are Nobel Prize for Peace, Literature, etc.; Goldman Environment Award; a merit scholarship.

ADDITIONAL WORDS CONCERNING FAMOUS PEOPLE

assassinate	polio
civil rights	religious
generation	segregated
hurdle	shy
inauguration	social cause
indigenous	soloist
orphanage	track and field

Questions

● What is the difference between *solo* and *soloist*?
● Where is the stress in these words: *assassinate, religious, indigenous, inauguration*?
● Label the words in this group according to their parts of speech. There are six nouns, one verb and four adjectives. Three words can be two parts of speech.
● What is a person called who lives in an *orphanage*?

Answers

① A *solo* is a piece of music performed by one musician; a *soloist* is the single musician.
② The stress is as follows: *assASSinate, relIGious, inDIGenous, inaugurAtion*.
③ *Generation, inauguration, orphanage, polio, social cause,* and *soloist* are nouns; *assassinate* is a verb; and *indigenous, religious, segregated,* and *shy* are adjectives. *Civil rights* and *track and field* can be used both as nouns and adjectives; *hurdle* can be both noun and verb.
④ An *orphan*.

PART 2: WORD EXTENSIONS

Synonyms

The more vocabulary you have to describe people, the better your descriptions will be. Practice reviewing words with similar meanings by matching the meanings of words on the left with the meanings of words on the right.

HINT   Make sure you match word forms as well as meaning.

talented	alone
start	achievement
solo	timid
brave	struggle
speak out for	courageous
shy	intelligent
fight	skillful
dedicated	committed
accomplishment	represent
smart	begin

Antonyms

Now match the following words with those in the antonym boxes. Write the word with the opposite meaning in the correct box. Be sure that both words are the same form.

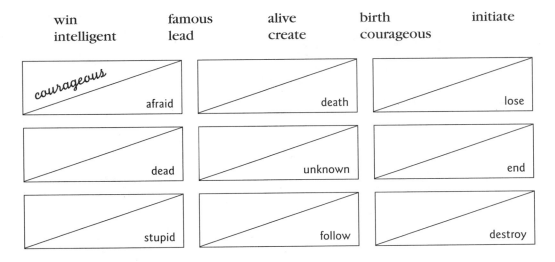

| win | famous | alive | birth | initiate |
| intelligent | lead | create | courageous | |

courageous — afraid

____ death

____ lose

____ dead

____ unknown

____ end

____ stupid

____ follow

____ destroy

Word Forms: Verbs to Nouns

Many verbs have noun forms. For example, *compete* is a verb. *Jackie Joyner-Kersee has competed in track and field events all her life.* You can turn the verb into a noun by knowing the correct form: *competition. Jackie Joyner-Kersee has done well in international competition.*

Several suffixes that change verbs to nouns are listed on the left. Write the noun forms of the verbs in the middle column. The first one is done for you.

SUFFIX	VERB	NOUN
-ition	compete	*competition*
-ation	explore	_____
	create	_____
	educate	_____
	inspire	_____
	initiate	_____
-ance	perform	_____
-ment	establish	_____
	improve	_____

Use Words Creatively

Personalizing: Making personal connections with people you're studying increases your motivation to learn.

1. Write a paragraph about a famous person who interests you. You can write about a person you've read about in this chapter or someone else. Use words from the Word Bank.

2. In groups of three or four, make a chart of famous twentieth-century men, like the one on page 26. If possible, go to the library to learn about each man's birth, background, activities, and accomplishments. Present your chart to the rest of the class when you are finished.

3. In groups of three or four, make a chart of famous *twenty-first* century people. Since you will be guessing, include their birth, background, and accomplishments and omit their names. Present your chart to the rest of the class when you are finished.

4. In a short presentation to your class, share some information about yourself. Include your birth and background, and explain what accomplishments you would like people to remember you for.

Word Games

Understanding and Using Emotions: Dramatizing to communicate information is a fun way to learn.

WHO AM I?

Pretend that you are a famous person. If possible, dress up like this person. Help your classmates guess who you are by talking about your background and famous achievements.

PASSWORD

Work in two teams. Put four chairs at the front of the room, two facing away from the chalkboard (towards the class) and two facing the chalkboard. Team members face each other. The teacher or a student selects a word from the Word Bank and writes it on the board. Students facing the board read the word silently and alternate giving one-word clues to their teammates.

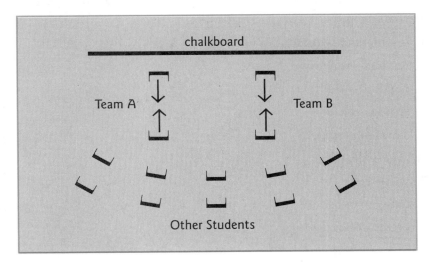

The first person to guess the word wins points for his or her team. Students get ten chances to guess the word. Points decrease with each turn. Students change places each time a new word is written on the board. The team with the most points at the end wins.

Recycle

Do at least one of the following activities in small groups. Combine words from this chapter with words from previous chapters.

1. Plan a face-to-face meeting with a living famous woman you admire. Where are you, what do you say, and how do you feel?
2. You are an editor for a book publishing company. You would like to work on the biography of a famous woman. Propose the woman whose biography will sell lots of books.
3. You are president of the Chamber of Commerce for your hometown. Every ten years, your local government gives an award to one woman who has made an important contribution to your community. They have asked you to recommend someone for this award. Think of a woman from your community and explain why she deserves this award.

Optional: Write your answers to the Recycle activities.

Review

Are the following pairs of words synonyms or antonyms? Write S if the words are similar in meaning and O if they are opposites.

_____ **1.** courageous—afraid

_____ **2.** famous—unknown

_____ **3.** talented—skillful

_____ **4.** strong—weak

_____ **5.** smart—intelligent

_____ **6.** alive—dead

_____ **7.** win—lose

_____ **8.** native—indigenous

_____ **9.** brave—courageous

_____ **10.** start—initiate

_____ **11.** lead—follow

_____ **12.** solo—alone

Threads

[I]n a sad world where so many are victims, I can take pride that I am also a fighter. My life, my career, every song I sing and every appearance I make, are bound up with the plight of my people.

Miriam Makeba,
singer South Africa

Test Yourself

Use the following words to complete the summary paragraph on famous women.

talented	courage	dreams
inspires	improve people's lives	skillful
face difficulties	dedication	famous
struggle		

Why do certain women become famous? There are many reasons. First, they may come from families that are already _____ . Or they meet someone who _____ them. Perhaps they want to make changes or _____ . Some women become famous because they are _____ or _____ . Many famous women _____ in their lives. Their roles as daughters, wives, and mothers may not encourage them to become famous. Some women _____ to achieve their _____ . Their _____ and their _____ help them.

34

Look Back

What did you learn about famous twentieth-century women in this chapter?

_____

_____

_____

_____

_____

Look Ahead

What else do you want to learn about famous people? How do you plan to do it?

_____

_____

_____

_____

_____

People: How Do You Learn Best?

PEOPLE: HOW DO YOU LEARN BEST?

Have you noticed that you are good at things other people are not? And have you found that you can't do what may be easy and natural for others? In this chapter you will explore a popular theory about some of the differences between people— how they learn.

PART 1: WORDS IN CONTEXT

Take a Look

People learn in different ways. In these photos, each person is trying to learn sports vocabulary. Look at the photos and write a sentence about how each of them is learning.

1. **EXAMPLE** *She's reading the list and repeating the words.*

2. _____

3. _____

4. _____

5. _____

_____

6. _____

_____

1. In which photo is the learner using his/her body (is physically active)?
2. In which photo is the learner alone?
3. In which photo is the learner with other people?
4. Which photos show types of learning that are similar?
5. Which ways of learning in the photos would **you** choose?

Personalizing: Applying your opinions to new learning materials will make the learning more meaningful.

Read About It

Read the following information on kinds of intelligences. This appeared in a college textbook.

We call people intelligent if they can solve problems in their lives and if they can make things that are valuable in their culture. There are at least seven types of intelligence—distinct ways we learn and know about reality, and there may be more. Although we can learn different forms of intelligence, every person has one primary type of intelligence, or way of knowing, that is most natural.

Threads

Herodotus lived in the 5th century B.C. and was the first Greek historian. Everywhere he went he studied the manners, customs, religions, and history of the people he visited. He is well-known for his lively (and exaggerated) historical accounts.

Forming Concepts: Changing the format of new material helps some learners learn faster.

7 Types of Intelligence

7 Ways of Knowing

Logical/Mathematical Intelligence deals with numbers, patterns, and inductive and deductive thinking. It is often called "scientific thinking."

Visual/Spatial Intelligence relies on sight and the ability to visualize an object.

Body/Kinesthetic Intelligence is based on physical movement and knowledge of the body.

Musical/Rhythmic Intelligence is based on the relationships and recognition of patterns in tones, sounds and on a sensitivity to rhythm and beats.

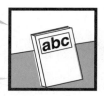

Verbal/Linguistic Intelligence is related to written and spoken words and language.

Intrapersonal Intelligence includes self-reflection and thinking about thinking.

Interpersonal Intelligence involves person-to-person communication.

Check Your Understanding

Use the seven types of intelligence listed to complete the exercises that follow.

a. Logical/Mathematical Intelligence

b. Verbal/Linguistic Intelligence

c. Visual/Spatial Intelligence

d. Intrapersonal Intelligence

e. Body/Kinesthetic Intelligence

f. Interpersonal Intelligence

g. Musical Rythmic Intelligence

Certain activities are easy for people with certain types of intelligence. Which intelligence do these activities favor? Write the letter of the corresponding type of intelligence next to each activity. You may find more than one answer.

_____ **1.** Working cooperatively in a group

_____ **2.** Teaching

_____ **3.** Playing the piano

_____ **4.** Mimicking an actor

_____ **5.** Keeping a daily journal of personal growth and experience

_____ **6.** Understanding others' nonverbal communication

_____ **7.** Recognizing a melody from a well-known opera

_____ **8.** Representing ideas in pictures

_____ **9.** Convincing someone to do something

_____ **10.** Performing complex mathematical or scientific calculations

Which intelligence do the following people favor? Write the letter of the corresponding type of intelligence next to each description.

_____ **11.** Jean-Pierre often connects a piece of music with an event in his life.

_____ **12.** Leila likes to study the structure and logic of languages.

_____ **13.** Norm enjoys doing puzzles and playing games.

_____ **14.** Alex likes to listen to a good speech, lecture, or sermon.

_____ **15.** Nicolas learns new dance steps fast.

_____ **16.** Sarah is always aware of how she feels.

_____ **17.** Hiroko has a good sense of balance and coordination.

_____ **18.** Sherif always knows north from south wherever he is.

_____ **19.** Caroline likes to work with numbers and figures.

_____ **20.** Peter is sensitive to other people's moods.

Overcoming Limitations: Applying new ideas to familiar situations extends and deepens your learning.

Word Bank

Here are the new words for this chapter. They are organized into three groups. Study the new words and add them to your Word Journal.

TYPES OF INTELLIGENCE

body	kinesthetic	primary
deductive	linguistic	rhythmic
distinct	logical	spatial
inductive	mathematical	valuable
interpersonal	musical	verbal
intrapersonal	natural	visual

HOW WE LEARN

face	recognize	is based on
favor	solve	is related to
include	visualize	involves
involve	deals with	relies on
produce		

ADDITIONAL WORDS FOR DESCRIBING INTELLIGENCE

beat	pattern	self-reflection
communication	reality	sensitivity
intelligence	relationship	tone
knowledge	rhythm	

Managing Your Learning: Organizing new words in different ways expands your understanding of them.

Questions

1. Write the correct part of speech above each group of words in the Word Bank.
2. There are nine four-syllable words in Groups 1, 2, and 3 of your Word Bank. First, find these nine words. Then mark the stressed syllable for each word.
3. One of the words in Group 1 can also be another part of speech. Which word is this and to which other group would you add it?
4. The middle part of the word *spatial* is pronounced like which of these words: *should, judge,* or *church*?
5. The second syllable in *produce* (Group 2) is stressed because it's a verb. But this word can also be a noun if the stress is on a different syllable. Pronounce this word as a noun.

Answers

① Group 1 words are adjectives, Group 2 are verbs, and Group 3 are nouns.
② Here are the stressed syllables of the nine words: interPERsonal, intraPERsonal, kinesTHETic, matheMATical, communiCAtion, reALity, reLAtionship, self-reFLECtion, and sensiTIVity.
③ *Body* in Group 1 can also be a noun (Group 3).
④ The middle sound of *spatial* is pronounced /sh/ as in *should.*
⑤ *PROduce* is a noun and it refers to fresh fruit and vegetables.

PART 2: WORD EXTENSIONS

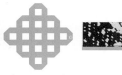

Prefixes

Prefixes are word parts that appear at the beginning of a word. You can use your understanding of prefixes to learn new words. Study this chart, and then answer the questions.

PREFIX	MEANING	EXAMPLE	YOUR EXAMPLES
inter-	between, among	interpersonal	
intra-	within	intrapersonal	
in-	in	inductive	
de-	down, reversing	deductive	
re-	again	reflection	

1. How many additional words with these prefixes can you think of? Write more examples in the last column.
2. How are the meanings of *international* and *interpersonal* similar?
3. *Reflection* has at least two definitions. It can mean a quiet thought or the appearance of your image in a mirror. How does *again,* the meaning of the prefix, help you understand similarities in these definitions?
4. Explain the difference between *interpersonal* and *intrapersonal* to a classmate.
5. Label these diagrams correctly. One shows *deductive* thinking—moving from one idea to many ideas. The other shows *inductive* thinking—moving from many ideas to one idea.

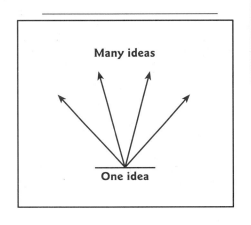

Threads

In 1983, Barbara McClintock won the *Nobel Prize in Medicine or Physiology* for her work in microbiology. Her intellectual powers of deduction and observation illustrate one form of Logical-Mathematical Intelligence that is often labeled "scientific thinking."

Word Origins

The meanings of words develop over time. It is often easier to remember word meanings when we know how they have developed. Study the origins of these words from the Word Bank.

kinesthetic: from the Greek word, *kinein,* which means *to move*
rhythmic: from Greek *rhuthmos,* which means *pattern*
spatial: from Latin *spatium,* meaning *space*
beat: from Middle Eastern *beten,* meaning *to strike repeatedly*
primary: from Latin *primus,* meaning *first*
verbal: from Latin *verbum,* meaning *word*
face: from Latin *facias,* meaning *top* or *surface*
body: from Old English *bodig,* meaning *shape*
intelligence: from Latin *intelligens,* to *perceive*

1. Where did most of the words in this list originate? Do you think this is true of English in general?
2. A comprehensive dictionary will give you word origins. Look up the origins of these three words: *logical, mathematical, musical.*

Word Forms: Nouns, Verbs, Adjectives

Many of the words in this chapter have different forms that correspond to different parts of speech. Work with a partner to complete this chart using words from the Word Bank. You'll notice that some words only have two forms with related meanings.

WORD FORMS		
NOUNS	VERBS	ADJECTIVES
	reflect	reflective
	X	rhythmic
	sense	sensitive
verb	verbalize	
X	visualize	
solution	solve	X
music	X	
distinction	distinguish	
	X	intelligent

Use Words Creatively

1. Read Amal's schedule of activities from last week. She recorded them according to the type of intelligence they favored. Read Amal's schedule with a partner, and then make five true statements about Amal.

AMAL'S WEEKLY SCHEDULE							
	Monday	Tuesday	Wednesday	Thursday	Friday	Saturday	Sunday
Logical/Math.			Pay bills				
Verbal/Linguistic	Write letter home					Go to library	
Visual/Spatial				Visit Museum			
Intrapersonal							Write in journal
Body/Kines.	Exercise at gym	Folk Dance Class	Play volleyball	Folk Dance Class	Go dancing		
Interpersonal							
Musical/Rhythmic		Practice piano				Rock concert	

2. Think about the things you've done in the past week and how the activities correspond to the seven types of intelligence. Jot down these activities as Amal has done in the previous exercise. When you are finished, share your completed schedule with a classmate. Does your schedule clearly favor one type of intelligence?

_____'S WEEKLY SCHEDULE						
	Monday	Tuesday	Wednesday	Thursday	Friday	Saturday	Sunday
Logical/Math.							
Verbal/Linguistic							
Visual/Spatial							
Intrapersonal							
Body/Kines.							
Interpersonal							
Musical/Rhythmic							

LEARNING STRATEGY

Understanding and Using Emotions: Thinking about the type of learning that you feel passionate about will probably help you understand how you learn best.

3. Write a paragraph about your primary intelligence. Give examples of what you learn best and fastest. Read your paragraph aloud to the class.

4. Look at a recent test you or a friend has taken for a class. What type of intelligence does this test favor? Present your results to your classmates. Then suggest what might be on the test to favor different types of intelligence.

5. Think about the educational system in your country. Does it favor one type of intelligence or does it provide opportunities for students with different kinds of intelligence to do well? Present your opinions with examples to your class in a short presentation.

Word Games

SPELLING BEE

Have an old-fashioned Spelling Bee. Your class will divide into two teams. One student (or the teacher) will read words from the Word Bank, one at a time, to students on alternating teams. Your team will earn one point for each correctly spelled word. The team with the most points at the end of the Spelling Bee wins.

GAMES AND INTELLIGENCE

Here's a game about games. Make a list of games you play, have played, or know about. What types of intelligence do they favor? (Some games may favor several types of intelligence.) Give your reasons for each answer. Begin with this list. Then add some more games of your own. The first student or team that can find at least one game for each of the seven types of intelligence wins.

GAMES	TYPES OF INTELLIGENCE	WHY?
Chess		
Musical Chairs		
Video Games		
Dominoes		
Mancala		
Crossword Puzzles		
Charades		

Recycle

Do at least one of the following activities in small groups. Combine words from this chapter with words from previous chapters.

1. What are the best places in your community for studying? Describe two places where you go to prepare for your classes.
2. Review the famous women you studied in Chapter 4. Can you find a connection between certain women and types of intelligence?
3. Pretend you are a futurist—that is, an expert on the future. You have been asked to speak to a group of high school graduates about the type(s) of intelligence that will be necessary for the jobs of the future. What will you say?

Optional: Write your answers to the Recycle activities.

PART 4: ASSESSMENT

Review

Your teacher is planning her classes for next week and she wants to be sure she includes activities for all intelligence types. Read the activities, write the type of intelligence it favors, and explain your answer.

CLASS ACTIVITIES	TYPE OF INTELLIGENCE	WHY?
1. Students draw a picture of what they have read		
2. Students talk to each other about a story they're reading		
3. Students analyze similarities and differences of grammar rules		
4. Students perform a skit		
5. Students use colored markers to highlight words they want to learn		
6. Students learn a song to practice a grammar structure		
7. Students write a story in teams		
8. Students give an oral presentation of their backgrounds and goals		
9. Students write poems with new words that rhyme		

Test Yourself

Use these words to complete the summary of multiple intelligences.

verbal/linguistic logical/mathematical body/kinesthetic
visual/spatial musical/rhythmic interpersonal
intrapersonal recognize relationships
patterns

There are many ways that the human mind shows its intelligence. There are at least seven distinct ways we learn and know about reality. _____ intelligence is responsible for the production of language and all its complex possibilities: poetry, humor, storytelling, writing. _____ intelligence involves the ability to _____ patterns and see _____. This is often called "scientific thinking."

_____ intelligence often belongs to mapmakers, architects, and artists. These people can form pictures in their mind.

_____ intelligence uses the body to learn and understand. Actors, clowns, and dancers often display this type of intelligence. _____ intelligence includes the ability to recognize _____ in tone and rhythm. People with this kind of intelligence are often good language learners. They are also sensitive to sounds in the environment.

_____ intelligence involves working well in groups with other people. Counselors, teachers, politicians, and religious leaders are often developed in this type of intelligence. These people are good at cooperation.

Finally, _____ intelligence involves self-knowledge. This intelligence is the most private and personal.

Look Back

What did you learn about types of intelligence from this chapter?

_____

_____

_____

_____

_____

Look Ahead

What else do you want to learn about types of intelligence? How do you plan to do it?

_____

_____

_____

_____

_____

Food: What Would You Like to Eat?

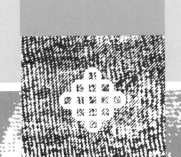

FOOD: WHAT WOULD YOU LIKE TO EAT?

Do you prepare your meals or do you eat out? Perhaps you do both. In this chapter, you will study words and expressions describing food that you might find in a restaurant or shopping mall.

PART 1: WORDS IN CONTEXT

Take a Look

Threads

In Mexico, *frijoles refritos*, or refried beans, are served with practically every meal. By putting a bit of bacon fat in the frying pan, they can be heated over and over again— improving each time.

Look at the following photos of ethnic food popular in the United States. With a partner, write the name of the food and where it comes from.

1. _____   2. _____

_____   _____

3. _____   4. _____   5. _____

_____   _____   _____

1. Which foods can you buy in your town or at your school?

_____

2. Which foods can you prepare?

_____

3. Add two more ethnic foods you might eat for lunch or dinner.

_____

Personalizing: Adding your own information to new material makes the new material more meaningful.

Read About It

Which ethnic food would you like to eat? The International Food Court at a large shopping mall sells meals from all over the world. Read the signs from each of the mini-restaurants then answer the questions.

THE ITALIAN EATERY
Savory Pizza
THICK or THIN Crust
Samples Cheerfully Given

¡LA SALSA!
Gourmet Mexican Specialties
Favorite dishes—Combinations
Low Cal Combo
Burritos—Fajitas

MONTEREY PASTA COMPANY
Eat Pasta for Life!
3 times a week! It's healthy!
Any three items $3.99
(Frequent Buyer Program)

THE SANDWICH EXPRESS
Sumptuous Sandwiches
Daily Specials

LE BON PAIN SOURDOUGH FRENCH BREAD BAKERY
Old Fashioned Bread Since 1849
Original recipe • Baked daily
(Gift Certificates available)

EMPEROR'S GARDEN
Fresh Chinese
(List of ingredients available at counter)
Kids' Menu

CHICAGO HOT DOGS
Delicious and Juicy
Char-broiled hamburgers

SWISS SWEET FACTORY
Classic Candy and Chocolate
$1.75 per quarter pound
Sugar-free, Fat-free varieties available

SUSHI MARU
Our sushi is cooked: boiled, grilled, or smoked.
Some of our sushi is marinated; some of our sushi is raw.
Lots of our sushi is vegetarian.
Highest Quality Seafood

Check Your Understanding

Answer these questions about the International Food Court.

1. What are the two kinds of pizza available at The Italian Eatery?
2. How many items can you get for $3.99 at The Monterey Pasta Company?
3. What is the name of the candy store?
4. Which restaurant has a French name?
5. What are the three ways sushi is cooked?
6. What do you think you can buy to eat at the Swiss Sweet Factory?
7. Which business at the International Food Court might be the oldest?
8. Which restaurant has a Frequent Buyer Program? What do you think that means?
9. Where could you eat if you're on a diet?
10. Where could you eat if you're a vegetarian?

Threads

Although *pasta* is popular in many cultures, the Italians have elevated it to an honored position. Each region of Italy has its own traditional *pasta* dish, and every Italian takes great pleasure in pointing out that there is no ingredient anywhere that cannot somehow be used in it, over it, or with it.

Forming Concepts: Reviewing new material for specific information helps you learn new words quickly.

11. If you were at International Food Court, where would you like to eat?
12. Where can you get a list of ingredients?
13. Where can you get samples of food without buying it?
14. Where can you buy gift certificates?
15. Match the name of the restaurant at the International Food Court with the type of food it probably serves.

Le Bon Pain Bakery   American
Monterey Pasta Company French
¡La Salsa!   Italian
The Italian Eatery   Chinese
Chicago Hot Dogs   Japanese
The Sandwich Express Mexican
Emperor's Garden   Swiss
Swiss Sweet Factory
Sushi Maru

Word Bank

Here are the new words from this chapter. Study them and answer the questions. Then add the new words to your Word Journal.

EATING OUT

available	dish	item	pizza	special
baked	eatery	juicy	popular	specialty
boiled	ethnic	low-cal	raw	sugar-free
char-broiled	fat-free	mall	recipe	sumptuous
classic	favorite	marinated	salsa	sweet
combination	fresh	meal	sample	take out
cooked	gourmet	menu	savory	thick
counter	grilled	old fashioned	seafood	thin
daily	healthy	original	smoked	varieties
delicious	ingredients	pasta	sour	vegetarian
dining				

LEARNING STRATEGY

Managing Your Learning: Guessing the kinds of questions you will be asked helps you learn faster.

Questions

❶ The words in the Word Bank are either nouns or adjectives. Rearrange the words in two lists according to their parts of speech.
❷ One word belongs in both groups. Which word is this?
❸ How many syllables does each of these words have: *mall, meal, sumptuous, recipe, savory, grilled, cooked, special, varieties?*
❹ In which word do you pronounce the *i* differently: *gift, item, dish, thick?*
❺ *Char-broiled* and *low-cal* are shortened forms of words. What do *char* and *cal* represent?
❻ What is *seafood?*
❼ Is the *th* in *the* and *thin* pronounced the same or differently?

Answers

1. Nouns: *combination, counter, dining, dish, eatery, ingredients, item, mall, meal, pasta, pizza, recipe, salsa, sample, seafood, special, specialty, varieties*
   All the other words are adjectives.
2. *Special* is both a noun and an adjective.
3. *Mall, grilled, cooked, meal* have one syllable; *special* has two syllables; *sumptuous, recipe,* and *savory* have three syllables; *varieties* has four syllables.
4. The *i* in *item* is pronounced /aɪ/, while in the other words it is pronounced /ɪ/.
5. *Charcoal* and *calorie.*
6. Fish and shellfish
7. They are pronounced differently: the *th* in *the* is voiced (that is, your vocal chords move); the *th* in *thin* is voiceless (your vocal chords do not move). Practice with these words from the Word Bank: *ethnic, thick, thin.*

PART 2: WORD EXTENSIONS

Associated Meanings

Look at these groups of words with similar meanings. One word in each group does not have an associated, or similar, meaning. Circle this word, and then talk about how the other words in the group are related.

EXAMPLE boiled   smoked   grilled   (ethnic)   baked

Ethnic does not fit in this group.
It is the only word that does not refer to a way to cook food.

1. dish   meal   juicy   specialty   combination

2. sweet   sumptuous   gourmet   thin   delicious

3. available   ethnic   international around-the-world

4. items   counter   ingredients   samples

5. take out   for here   sugar-free   to go

6. pizza   pasta   sushi   daily   burrito

7. favorite   sugar-free   fat-free   low-cal

8. eatery   food court   restaurant   marinated

LEARNING STRATEGY

Remembering New Material: Identifying other words that have similar meanings makes it easier to remember the meanings of new words.

Using *Since*

Use *since* to indicate that something began in the past and is still occurring. Use the present perfect (*have* + past participle) or the present perfect progressive (*have* + *been* + present participle) form of the verb and include a specific time.

EXAMPLES The Le Bon Pain Bread Bakery has been selling fresh bread *since* 1849.

Char-broiled Teriyaki with Ota-San's gourmet Teriyaki Sauce has been available *since* last month.

Uncle Eric has been a vegetarian *since* November 1995.

The International Food Court has been serving ethnic specialities *since* 1990.

Practice using *since* by answering these questions.

1. How long have you been eating different kinds of food?
2. How long have you been studying this chapter?
3. Have you been eating pasta for a long time?
4. How long have you been cooking your own food?

Now ask and answer a question of your own.

Threads

Stir-frying is quick cooking and stirring of foods in a tiny amount of oil over high heat. This one cooking method is uniquely Chinese.

Antonyms

Match the following words with those in the antonym boxes. Put the word with the opposite meaning in the correct box. Be sure that both words are the same form.

raw	fresh	available	thick
sour	juicy	buyer	low-cal

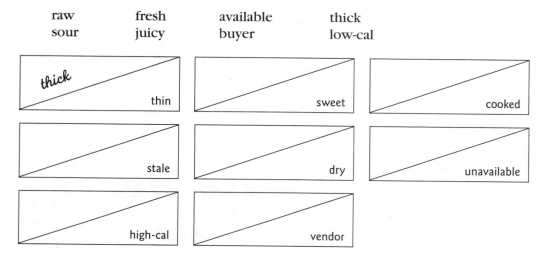

thick / thin

/ sweet

/ cooked

/ stale

/ dry

/ unavailable

/ high-cal

/ vendor

Use Words Creatively

1. In small groups, take turns talking about the food you like to eat. Could you buy your favorite food at the International Food Court? Is there a mall or restaurant nearby where you can buy your favorite food?

LEARNING STRATEGY

Understanding and Using Emotions: Using persuasive language and strong feelings helps convey your point of view to other people.

2. Add a new and different restaurant to the International Food Court. Give the restaurant a name. What kind of food does it serve? Where does the food come from? Make a sign for the new restaurant. Use language that will make your classmates want to come and eat there. If possible, bring samples of the food your restaurant will serve.

3. Visit an ethnic restaurant in town and present an oral or written report of your meal there.

4. If there is a mall in your town, compare the restaurants in your mall with the International Food Court. Consider prices, number of restaurants, and availability of ethnic food.

Word Games

STORY CHAIN

Sit in a circle and build a story by recalling what each person ate for lunch yesterday or today. Begin like this:

First student: I ate *a burrito* for lunch today.

Second student: I ate *a burrito* and *a piece of pizza* for lunch today.

Third student: I ate *a burrito, a piece of pizza,* and *sushi* for lunch today.

Continue like this for 15 minutes. If you complete the circle and there is time left, add adjectives (I ate a *delicious* burrito today.) Try to remember what everyone ate.

WHERE SHOULD I EAT?

In pairs, use adjectives and expressions from this chapter to help a classmate guess the right restaurant at the International Food Court. The person who is "It" will use your clues to guess the name of the restaurant.

Player 1: You want to eat something Italian.

Player 2: I want pasta at the Monterey Pasta Factory.

Player 1: No. You want to eat something Italian and you want to try a free sample first.

Player 2: I want pizza at The Italian Eatery.

Player 1: Yes.

Then, players switch roles and continue in this way.

Recycle

Do at least one of the following activities in small groups. Combine words from this chapter with words from previous chapters.

1. Are there certain foods that make you smart? Talk about food myths and realities related to intelligence.
2. You have been asked to design a food court for your community. Where would it go and what kinds of food would you offer? Consider foods that are popular (but not already available) in the area where you live. Sketch a plan for your food court and present it to the class.
3. Think of a famous woman who will be the symbol for a new line of products. The products should reflect the woman and her values. Explain why this woman will make the product more popular.

Optional: Write your answers to the Recycle activities.

 **PART 4: ASSESSMENT**

Review

Complete the sentences by choosing the appropriate word. Use each word once.

| eatery | daily | meal | take out | raw |
| sour | sumptuous | counter | vegetarian | sweet |

1. _____ meals have no meat.
2. If you want to take your food home to eat, you ask for _____.
3. You often pay for your food at the _____.
4. If sandwiches are made every day, they are fresh _____.
5. Before food is cooked, it is _____.

6. A place to eat can be called an _____ .

7. A dish can refer to a plate or a _____ .

8. Many _____ foods use sugar as an ingredient.

9. _____ means "grand."

10. French bread can be made with _____ dough.

Test Yourself

Complete the following radio commercial for the International Food Court.

| low-cal combo | kids' menu | gourmet | sushi | daily specials |
| ethnic | Chinese | varieties | delicious | favorite |

Everyone in the family likes different food? No problem! Just head on down to the International Food Court where everyone can find their _____ food in the same place. There are more than
₁

six _____ of _____ _____
₂   ₃   ₄

food at the International Food Court. Uncle Eric loves _____ ,
₅

so he can eat at Sushi Maru. Dad wants a ham sandwich. He can find one on

the list of _____ at The Sandwich Express. Susie, age 8,
₆

likes _____ food. She can choose something from a
₇

_____ at Emperor's Garden.
₈

Grandma wants a hot dog and Cousin Linda who's on a diet will have the

_____ at ¡La Salsa! There's something for everyone at the
₉

International Food Court, so hurry on down to your headquarters for

_____ food from around the world.
₁₀

Look Back

What did you learn about international dining in this chapter?

_____

_____

_____

_____

_____

Look Ahead

What else do you want to learn about international dining? How will you do this?

_____

_____

_____

_____

Food: What's In It?

We all love to eat, but we don't always think about what's *in* the food we eat. In this chapter, you're going to talk and write about food, food additives, and how food is made or grown.

PART 1: WORDS IN CONTEXT

Take a Look

Look at the food in each photo. In small groups, answer these questions about each item:

1. What is it?
2. What's in it? Is there anything in it besides food? What?
   (Just guess—See Item "a" as an example.)
3. Was it manufactured (made in a factory) or grown? How?
   (Just guess—See Item "a" as an example.)

b.

1. _____
2. _____
3. _____

c.

1. _____
2. _____
3. _____

a.

1. _____ *soft drink* _____
2. _____ *artificial color* _____
3. _____ *manufactured* _____

d.

1. _____
2. _____
3. _____

e.

1. _____
2. _____
3. _____

Overcoming Limitations: Using new words to make guesses about familiar objects helps you gain confidence.

Read About It

Read the information on these food packages:

Product 1

Sunnyside Eggs

One Dozen

From Chickens Raised without Cages • No Hormones or Antibiotics

Luigi's *Old Style*

Spaghetti Sauce

Only the Finest Natural Ingredients: Tomato Concentrate from Vine-ripened, Organically Grown Tomatoes, Soybean, Oil, Salt, Sugar, Spices, Olive Oil.

Product 2

ORGANIC · NATURAL · NO PESTICIDES

Product 3

HomeMade
EGG BREAD

NO PRESERVATIVES • NO ARTIFICIAL COLORS OR FLAVORS
Ingredients: Enriched Wheat Flour (Wheat Flour, Niacin, Iron, Thiamin, Riboflavin), Water, Eggs, Honey, Nonfat Milk, Yeast, Sea Salt, Soybean Oil.

NEW! # Pilgrim Brand
CHEWY
GRANOLA BARS

ORIGINAL FLAVOR
10 BARS

Ingredients: Rolled oats, brown sugar, vegetable oil, nonfat dry milk, honey, corn syrup, natural and artificial flavors, BHT (a preservative).

Product 4

Check Your Understanding

Managing Your Learning: Working with a partner increases your chances for acquiring new information.

Work with a partner and answer these questions about the food labels:

1. Which products do not have any artificial (nonfood) ingredients? Give three examples of ingredients that are not artificial.
2. Which products have artificial ingredients? Give two examples of artificial ingredients.
3. Look at Sunnyside Eggs (Product 1). What kind of chickens did these eggs come from? How were they raised?
4. Look at Luigi's Spaghetti Sauce (Product 2). What kind of tomatoes are in this sauce? How were they grown?
5. Look at HomeMade Egg Bread (Product 3). What do you think *enriched* wheat flour is?
6. Look at Pilgrim Brand Granola Bars (Product 4). What kind of sugar is in this product? Are any other sweeteners (things that make food sweet) in the granola bars? If so, what are they?
7. What is BHT?
8. What does *vine-ripened* mean?
9. What are hormones? What kind of food might you find them in?

Word Bank

Here are the new words for this chapter. Add them to your Word Journal.

FOOD

soybean oil	egg	(rolled) oats
vegetable oil	honey	corn syrup
olive oil	(nonfat/dry) milk	apple
tomato	(brown) sugar	fruit
wheat flour	(sea) salt	(soft) drink
spice	yeast	ice cream
spaghetti sauce	granola bar	

FOOD ADDITIVES (NONFOOD INGREDIENTS)

hormone	niacin
antibiotic	iron
thiamin	BHT
riboflavin	preservative
artificial color	artificial flavor
additive	ingredient
vitamin	mineral

FOOD PROCESSING (HOW FOOD IS MADE)

to process	natural
to manufacture	concentrate
to grow	enriched (with vitamins and minerals)
organic	to sweeten
organically grown	to raise
vine-ripened	pesticide

Questions

❶ How many kinds of oil are in the **Food** list? What are they?

❷ Which three items in the **Food Additives** list are vitamins?

❸ Which item in the **Food Additives** list is a mineral?

❹ Where is the stress in the following words in the **Food Additives** list: *artificial, antibiotic, preservative?*

❺ Group the words in all three lists according to these parts of speech: nouns, verbs, adjectives, adverbs.

LEARNING STRATEGY

Overcoming Limitations: Learning how to pronounce new words helps you use them with confidence.

Answers

❶ There are three oils in the list: *soybean, olive,* and *vegetable.*

❷ *Riboflavin, niacin,* and *thiamin* are vitamins.

❸ The mineral is *iron.*

❹ Here's how you stress these words: artiFIcial, antibiOtic, preSERVAtive.

❺ Nouns: All the words under **Food** and **Food Additives** are nouns: *soybean oil, egg, (rolled) oats, pesticide, vegetable oil, honey, corn syrup, olive oil, nonfat (nonfat/dry) milk, tomato, (brown) sugar, wheat flour, (sea) salt, spice, yeast, spaghetti sauce, apple, fruit, (soft) drink, ice cream, granola bar, hormone, niacin, antibiotic, iron, thiamin, additive, BHT, riboflavin, preservative, artificial color, artificial flavor, ingredient, vitamin, mineral.* Two additional nouns from the **Food Processing** list are *pesticide* and *concentrate.* The rest of the words (mostly from the **Food Processing** list) are adjectives: *organic, organically grown, vine-ripened, natural,* and *enriched.* The verbs are: *to process, to manufacture, to grow, to raise, to sweeten.* There are no adverbs, but *organically grown* is a combination of an adverb (*organically*) and an adjective (*grown*).

Threads

Some ice cream contains propylene glycol alginate, a chemical used in paint remover.

The People's Almanac

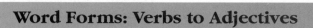
Word Forms: Verbs to Adjectives

You can extend your vocabulary by turning verbs into adjectives. When you want to use the adjective form of a verb, use its past participle form.

>   ***EXAMPLE***   *Processed* foods often have a lot of additives.

>   Here are the steps for getting the past participle of a regular verb:

>   to process ———> processed ———> (have, has) processed
>   Verb, Present Tense   Past Tense   Past Participle

>   Write the correct adjective form on the line next to each verb.

>   ***NOTE***   *Grown* is the past participle of *grow,* an irregular verb.

sweetened   vine-ripened   enriched
organically grown   processed

Verb	**Adjective**
to process	_____
to ripen on the vine	_____
to grow organically	_____
to enrich	_____
to sweeten	_____

LEARNING STRATEGY

Remembering New Material: Using new words immediately helps you remember their meanings.

Now use the adjective form of the verbs in parentheses to complete each of the following sentences:

1. _____ (to enrich) bread usually contains vitamins and minerals.

2. _____ (to process) foods don't taste as good as natural foods.

3. I buy _____ _____ (to grow organically) vegetables because I think they taste better.

4. People who want to avoid sugar, drink artificially _____ (to sweeten) drinks.

5. Sylvia only uses _____ (to ripen on the vine) tomatoes to make spaghetti sauce.

Word Associations

Overcoming Limitations: Doing word association exercises helps you extend your vocabulary quickly.

You can stretch your vocabulary if you think about all the additional words associated with a single word. Word associations also help you remember word meanings. Here's how you do it: Just take a cue word, for example *vegetable,* and say or write all the words it makes you think of: *lettuce, pea, bean, produce,* or *food,* etc.

Now try this with the following words from the Word Bank. Use these guidelines to make associations:

Think of words that are

- similar to the cue word in meaning or form
- examples of the cue word
- in the same category as the cue word

EXAMPLE
vegetable: lettuce, pea, bean, produce, food

natural: _____

organic: _____

processed: _____

spice: _____

artificial: _____

vitamin: _____

additive: _____

PART 3: USING WORDS

Use Words Creatively

1. Find a food product at home that has an interesting label and/or ingredients list. Study the label. Bring the food to school. In small groups, discuss the food you brought. As you discuss, answer these questions:
- What is it?
- What's in it?
- Which ingredients are natural? Which are artificial?
- How was it grown or processed?

2. In small groups, pretend you are a food manufacturing company. Create a new food product. Describe its ingredients and how it is manufactured, grown, or processed. Think of a name for your product. Then draw a package label for it that includes:
   • Your company name
   • The product name
   • Art that makes the product look attractive
   • An ingredients list
   • Other important information about the product that will make people want to buy it, such as *100% Natural* or *Organically Grown*.

3. Present your new product to the class. Be prepared to answer any questions your classmates might have about it.

4. Some people call processed food (food with a lot of additives) "junk food." Most people like to eat junk food some of the time because it's fun and it tastes good. In small groups, talk about the kinds of junk food you like to eat. Talk about what ingredients make it junk food.

Threads

Americans consume more than 4,460,000,000 cases of soft drinks each year.

Ethnic Almanac

Word Game

SCAVENGER HUNT

Get into two teams. Go to a supermarket and write the name of the food product that matches each of the following descriptions. The first team to complete the list correctly wins. Read each description with your teacher before you start.

Find a food product that:

1. Has soybean oil in it: _____

2. Contains artificial sweetener, artificial color, AND artificial flavor:

_____

3. Lists *sugar* as the first ingredient in the list of ingredients:

_____

4. Is made from an organic vegetable: _____

5. Says *100% Natural* on the label: _____

6. Has sea salt in it: _____

7. Is enriched with vitamins and minerals: _____

8. Says *processed* on the label: _____

9. Says *No Hormones* on the label: _____

10. Contains BHT: _____

Recycle

Do at least one of the following activities in small groups. Combine words from this chapter with words from previous chapters.

1. You are a travel agent. Some of your customers are going to travel long distances and use many forms of transportation. They are going to travel by air, by sea, by train, etc. Tell them what kind of food they can expect on each form of transportation.

2. Share with your group any information you have on famous women who work with food or food ingredients:
   - chefs
   - cooking teachers
   - cookbook authors
   - nutritionists
   - inventors
   - scientists

   Talk about their work: What did they create, write, invent, discover?
   Optional: Write your answers to the Recycle activities.

PART 4: ASSESSMENT

Review

LEARNING STRATEGY

Managing Your Learning: Timing yourself on a practice test helps increase your confidence.

Work with a partner. See how quickly you can match the definitions on the left with words from the Word Bank on the right. Record your time.

1. a kind of oil	pesticides
2. a kind of sweetener	BHT
3. an artificial ingredient	riboflavin
4. bread can be made from this	corn syrup
5. these tomatoes taste the best	organically grown
6. a vitamin	soybean
7. a preservative	enriched
8. this kills insects	color
9. grown without pesticides	wheat flour
10. flour that has vitamins and minerals	vine-ripened

Test Yourself

Complete the following food labels with these words from the Word Bank:

preservative   artificial   oil   ingredients
iron   soybean   organically enriched
sugar   nonfat

_____ :
1
_____ grown
2
tomatoes, olive _____ , salt.
3

Spaghetti Sauce

Grandma's
GRANOLA BARS

Ingredients:

Rolled oats, _____ oil,
4
brown _____ ,
5
_____ color,
6
artificial flavor, BHT (a _____)
7

WonderKids Bread

Ingredients: _____ wheat flour
8
(niacin, thiamin, riboflavin, _____),
9
_____ milk, sugar, salt, yeast.
10

100% Natural

Look Back

What did you learn about words that describe different kinds of food, food additives, and food processing?

_____

_____

_____

_____

_____

Look Ahead

What else do you want to learn about different kinds of food, food additives, and food processing? How do you plan to do this?

_____

_____

_____

_____

_____

_____

Fun: Why Do You Travel Abroad?

Some people travel to far away places to relax. Others travel to have adventures, work, or learn new things. In this chapter, you will discover different reasons to travel abroad.

PART 1: WORDS IN CONTEXT

Take a Look

Look at these travel ads:

Caribbean Ecotours. Bird watching, hiking, scuba diving, kayaking, and mountain biking adventures in Jamaica and Dominican Republic. Call CE Tours 800.555.1230 or 818.555.9169.

Spanish in Mexico. Only $250. Cost includes two weeks of classes. Individualized instruction, homestays with families, sports, field trips. Instituto Falco, Meteros #330, Morelia, MEXICO. Tel/Fax: (52) 43-14592.

Worldwide Internships. Be a camp counselor in the Netherlands, do community service in the United Kingdom, work on a farm in Norway. For information, contact Global Employment, 555 Bayard St., Pittsburgh, PA 15213.

Amazon. Rainforest expeditions, led by Margaret Sangiacomo. Travelers work on ecological projects, stay with local families, study exotic plants and animals. Only $1,975. Amazon Expeditions, 56478 Seastrand Parkway, Miami, FL 33461

Now discuss the following in small groups:

1. Where have you traveled? Where would you like to travel?
2. Why do you travel? To relax? To have an adventure? To learn about a new culture?
3. Have you ever worked in a foreign country? What did you do? What was it like?
4. Describe your most exciting travel experience.

Threads

When in Rome, do as the Romans do.

Read About It

Read the following excerpt about a student who had a travel adventure. Guess the meaning of any words you don't know.

Mary Stanski, a student at the University of Pennsylvania, traveled to India to study the culture and history of the country. While she was there, the Gulf War started, and her program was canceled. Instead of going home, she decided to travel around India and Tibet and learn by herself. She stayed with volunteers in Tibetan refugee camps, and with Indian families. During her travels, she learned about the political problems in Tibet. When she returned to the United States, she enrolled in Tibetan studies and language classes. She now helps Tibetan refugees who have come to live in the United States.

Check Your Understanding

Check your understanding of the passage you just read by filling in the following grid.

TRAVEL PROFILE
What was Mary Stanski's reason for going abroad? (Circle one)
To have an adventure　　　　To study　　　To relax　　　To work
Where did she go?
Who did she stay with?
What did she learn?
How did the travel experience change her life?

Word Bank

Here are the new words for this chapter. Add them to your Word Journal.

TRAVELING ABROAD

community service	expedition	cancel
ecological	adventure	project
enroll	exotic	bird watching
culture	local	scuba diving
history	native	kayaking
(the) Amazon	worldwide	mountain biking
refugee camp	political	study program
rainforest	abroad	camp counselor
vacation	volunteer	ecotour
tourism	internship	homestay
field trip	individualized instruction	

LEARNING STRATEGY

Overcoming Limitations: Analyzing new words helps you use them correctly.

Questions

1. What two words does *ecotour* come from?
2. What do these activity nouns (nouns that come from verbs) have in common: *bird watching, scuba diving, kayaking, mountain biking?*
3. What do these words have in common: *community service, bird watching, scuba diving, mountain biking, study program, camp counselor?*
4. How do you stress words like the ones in Question ❸?

Answers

1. Ecotour comes from *ecology* and *tour.*
2. They end in *-ing.*
3. They are two-word noun phrases. The first noun acts like an adjective—it describes the second noun.
4. Here's how you pronounce these words: comMUnity service, BIRD watching, SCUba diving, MOUNtain biking, STUdy program, CAMP counselor. In two-word noun phrases, you put the most stress on the normally stressed syllable of the first noun.

Word Forms: Nouns, Verbs, Adjectives, Adverbs

Many of the words in the Word Bank have related forms that are a different part of speech. For example, *ecological* is an adjective. When you add *-ly*, it becomes an adverb. There also are two noun forms: *ecology*, meaning the field, and *ecologist*, meaning the person who works in the field.

    Fill in the following word-form chart with the missing forms of the words from the Word Bank. Work in five teams. Each team fills in one of the part-of-speech columns: people nouns, thing nouns, verbs, adjectives, and adverbs.

    NOTE   An *X* means there is no form.

LEARNING STRATEGY

Forming Concepts: Analyzing word forms helps increase your vocabulary.

NOUNS: PEOPLE	NOUNS: THINGS OR FIELDS	VERBS	ADJECTIVES	ADVERBS
	adventure	X		X
	service		X	X
		X	ecological	
		enroll		X
	ecotour	X	X	X

Word Forms: *People* Nouns and *Thing* Nouns

Some of the nouns in the Word Bank refer to people and other nouns refer to things. Many of the *people* nouns have *thing* forms. For example, an *internship* is a period of time in which a person learns a new job while doing it. An *intern* is the person doing the internship.

You can sometimes make a "people noun" into a "thing noun" by adding an ending. The most common *thing* endings are: *-ing, -ism,* and *-ship*.

1. Working with a partner, fill in the chart with the missing *people* or *thing* forms of the following nouns.

PEOPLE NOUNS	THING NOUNS
volunteer	_____
_____	tourism
_____	mountain biking
counselor	_____
_____	scuba diving
_____	bird watching
_____	kayaking
intern	_____

2. Complete the following sentences with the correct form of the nouns from the previous chart:

   a. Mary got an _____ (intern/internship) at a big company in France; she won't get a salary, but she'll learn a lot about doing business in France.

   b. _____ (Scuba diver/Scuba diving) is an expensive sport: you need to buy a lot of equipment.

   c. A _____ (bird watcher/bird watching) will enjoy a vacation in Costa Rica; there's a lot of interesting wildlife in the rainforest.

   d. Mark worked as a _____ (volunteer/volunteerism) in a refugee camp last summer.

   e. I don't enjoy being a _____ (tourist/tourism) in a foreign country; I like to stay for awhile and learn how people actually live there.

3. Think of additional people nouns that become thing nouns when you add *-ing, -ism,* or *-ship*. Write them in your Word Journal.

Threads

A direct flight from Los Angeles to Irian Jaya, Indonesia, takes about 15 hours.

Structure: Infinitives of Purpose

You can travel abroad for many purposes. When you write or talk about reasons for traveling, you can use infinitives of purpose. An infinitive is a verb in the *to* form: *to go, to study, to travel*. For example, Mary Stanski went to India *to study* the history and culture of the country. Another way to say this is: Mary Stanksi went to India *in order to study* history and culture.

With a partner, practice using infinitives of purpose by completing the following sentences with the words in parentheses.

1. (volunteer/with refugee programs)
   Margaret went to Croatia _____
2. (go bird watching/in the rainforest)
   For my next vacation, I'm going to Costa Rica _____
3. (enroll in/ESL classes)
   Ping went to San Francisco _____
4. (learn/French)
   Adi went to France _____
5. (work/on a farm)
   Ken is going to Sweden this summer _____

LEARNING STRATEGY

Personalizing: Using new words to talk about yourself helps you remember them.

Now make up your own sentences about reasons for trips you have taken, or trips you would like to take. Use infinitives of purpose.

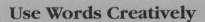 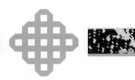

PART 3: USING WORDS

Use Words Creatively

1. In small groups, talk about your travel experiences. Talk about:
   • where you've traveled abroad
   • reasons you went to each place
   • what you learned there (if you learned something new)
   • what you did there that you had never done before
   • how the experience changed your life or your attitudes
2. Work in small groups. Choose one person to take notes (the notetaker), and one person to report on your group's answers (the reporter). Answer these questions:
   Imagine you can go anywhere in the world to do whatever you want. What kind of travel experience will you have? Why? Where will you go? Why? What will you do? Why?
   When you are finished talking, have the reporter tell your group's answers to the class.

Overcoming Limitations: Pretending you're someone else helps you use language creatively.

3. Pretend you are a travel agent. In an oral presentation, try to convince your classmates to travel somewhere. Give lots of reasons. Try to *sell* your travel idea: Bring pictures or make a travel poster. Bring examples of things you can find in the country or culture: music, art, clothing, products, etc.

4. Write a paragraph about one of the following:
   • Why do you like to travel abroad?
   • What is your ideal trip abroad?
   • Who is the ideal tourist?
   • Why would you recommend that someone visit _____ (name of country/region)?
   • Why is ecotourism popular nowadays?

Word Game

CHARADES WITH SOUND EFFECTS

Remembering New Material: *Playing* with new words makes remembering them easy.

Write these words (and word forms) from this chapter on 3 × 5 inch cards and put them face down on a table. Then form two teams. Have one team member pick a card and *act out* the job or activity on the card. Use sound effects, but do not speak. The goal is to get team members to guess the activity.

bird watching	kayaking	walking in a rainforest
scuba diving	mountain biking	studying
touring	eating new food	

Add your own travel activities.

Recycle

Do at least one of the following activities in small groups. Combine words from this chapter with words from previous chapters.

1. You are an experienced world traveler. Tell a group of students who are going to study abroad about the kinds of food they will find in some of the countries you have visited. Also talk about the ingredients and how the food is prepared or produced.
2. You are a tour guide in your city or town. Tell a group of tourists what kinds of transportation they should take to get from where you are to five different places abroad.

   Optional: Write your answers to the Recycle activities.

PART 4: ASSESSMENT

Review

Work with a partner. Review the meanings of words from this chapter by taking the following review quiz together:

1. Match the equipment on the left to the correct adventure vacation activity on the right:

oxygen tank	bird watching
binoculars	scuba diving
helmet	kayaking
paddle	mountain biking

2. *Trip* and *homestay*
   a. mean about the same thing
   b. have different meanings
3. *Local* and *native*
   a. mean about the same thing
   b. have different meanings
4. Which is an example of *community service?*
   a. helping repair roads
   b. studying art
   c. kayaking
5. Which of the following activities is most likely part of an *ecotour*?
   a. motorcycle racing
   b. bird watching
   c. shopping in department stores
6. Which of the following best describes a volunteer job?
   a. You don't get paid.
   b. You make a lot of money.
   c. You are the boss.
7. Why do some students probably choose a *homestay* when they study abroad?
   a. Because they like to be alone.
   b. Because they want to speak their native language.
   c. Because they want a lot of practice speaking the local language.
8. What is your *native* country?
   a. the country your parents were born in
   b. the country you were born in
   c. your favorite country

Test Yourself

Test your knowledge of the meanings of the words from this chapter by taking the following quiz. Read the letter. Then fill in the blanks with the words from the Word Bank, or forms of them. (There may be more than one possibility for some blanks.)

native	ecotour	abroad	study program
exotic	scuba diving	adventure	camp counselor
study	enrolling		

Dear Hiroko,

I don't think I'll see you for quite awhile because I'm going _____. I'm going to Costa Rica to
<u>1</u>
_____ Spanish and rainforest plants
<u>2</u>
and animals. I'm _____ in a
<u>3</u>
_____ that lasts four weeks. Then I have
<u>4</u>
a job for two weeks as a _____ in a camp
<u>5</u>
for children at a resort near the school. After that, I'm going on a rainforest
_____ to study _____
<u>6</u> <u>7</u>
plants and animals with _____
<u>8</u>
teachers. It's not all hard work, though. As part of the ecotour, we'll go
_____ to view the beautiful fish in
<u>9</u>
the Caribbean. It's going to be a real _____!
<u>10</u>

See you next year!
Keiko

Threads

Northeast Turkey gets
70 inches of rain a year.

Look Back

What did you learn about words that describe different reasons for traveling abroad?

_____

_____

_____

Look Ahead

What else do you want to learn about traveling abroad? How do you plan to do this?

_____

_____

_____

Fun: What Do You Do for Fun?

8

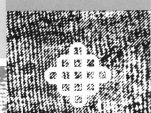

There are lots of places to go and things to do for fun. In this chapter, you will learn words and expressions for spending free time.

 PART 1: WORDS IN CONTEXT

Take a Look

Look at the following photos of people having fun. Write a sentence about what they are doing.

1. _____

_____

2. _____

_____

3. _____

_____

4. _____

_____

5. _____

6. _____

1. How many of the activities in the photos can people do alone?
2. How many of the activities involve birds or animals?
3. Which of the activities have you tried or would like to try?
4. Think of five more activities people do for fun.

LEARNING STRATEGY

Personalizing Your Learning: Applying your own experience to new material helps you use new words quickly.

Read About It

Read the following newspaper column. It reports what people said when they were asked what they like to do for fun.

Remy, the reporter with questions, asks:
What do you do for fun?

David, 29, Law Student. I spend all my free time going to movies. I really like foreign movies. I relax at the movies.

Christine, 22, Au Pair. I belong to a running club and we run every weekend. I run to stay fit and spend time with my friends. It's race season. Right now we're training for a marathon at the end of the month.

Wei, 45, Teacher. I read for fun. I read to improve my English and to learn things. I don't read as often as I'd like to—maybe a couple times a week. I have to be in a quiet place. The most interesting stories for me are about people who move to a new country. I feel encouraged by these stories.

Scott, 18, High School Student. I don't have any hobbies, so when I can find time and a buddy, I drive to the stock car races. They're exciting to watch and they take my mind off my worries. I do this about once a month in the spring and summer.

Dennis, 36, Mechanic. I enjoy fishing. I like to get out in nature where it's peaceful. It's fun to catch fish. I like eating what I catch. I try to go fishing at least once a month.

Aimée, 33, Bus Driver. I look through old things for fun whenever I visit my parents on the holidays. I spend hours going through photograph albums, stamp collections, my grandparents' letters and the antiques my family has saved. Looking through photo albums makes me feel grown up and mature. Some day I'll make a scrapbook for my children.

Check Your Understanding

1. Which of the people in the survey have fun alone? How many have fun with others?
2. Which people have fun and work towards self-improvement at the same time?
3. Complete the following chart with information from the newspaper column. Fill in the information for yourself at the bottom of the chart.

WHO?	WHAT?	WHY?	HOW OFTEN?
David	Goes to movies	It's relaxing	In his free time

4. What does Aimée's family collect? What are some other things that people collect for a hobby?

LEARNING STRATEGY

Managing Your Learning: Organizing new material into a chart helps you remember it.

Word Bank

FREE TIME

foreign	spend time	marathon
peaceful	belong to	nature
exciting	stay fit	album
mature	train for	club
quiet	take my mind off	column
grown up		worries
		hobbies
		buddy
		photos
		season
		member

Questions

1. Each column in the Word Bank is a different part of speech. Write the correct part of speech at the top of each column.
2. Is the final sound in *column* and *album* the same or different? Which letter in which word is silent?
3. Do *nature* and *mature* rhyme?
4. Which two words in the Word Bank have a singular form that ends in *-y*?
5. Which two words rhyme with *foreign*: <u>more in</u> or <u>more rain</u>?
6. Which word from the Word Bank describes people who belong either to a family or to a club?

Answers

6. *Member*
5. *More in*
4. *Hobby* and *worry.*
3. No. The stress is on different syllables, so the *a* is pronounced differently: NAture and maTURE.
2. The final sounds are the same. The *n* in *column* is silent.
1. Column 1: adjectives; Column 2: verbs; Column 3: nouns.

PART 2: WORD EXTENSIONS

Makes Me Feel . . .

LEARNING STRATEGY

Understanding and Using Emotions: Connecting experiences and feelings helps you remember new words.

People sometimes choose activities because of the way they make them feel. Study the columns of activities and feelings, then practice making sentences. Add words of your own to both columns.

> **EXAMPLE**   I like to read because it *makes me feel* relaxed.

Activities	Feelings	
play soccer	relaxed	grown up
go fishing	happy	excited
read	encouraged	anxious
travel	strong	nervous
study	happy	impatient
play basketball	fit	sleepy
go jogging		
collect coins		

Structure: Verbal Adjectives

Verbs that end in *-ed* or *-ing* can be used as adjectives. There are rules to help you use verbal adjectives correctly in sentences with the verb *to be*. Look at these examples:

I was bored by that movie.   That movie was boring.

- Use the *-ed* form of the verb when the subject *receives* the action. For example, in the first sentence, "I" receives the action.
- Use the *-ing* form when the subject *causes* the action. For example, in the second sentence, "movie" causes the action.

Practice making correct sentences with these pairs of words. The first one is done for you.

1. exciting/horse race
   Yesterday's horse race was very exciting.
   _____

2. frightened/horror movie
   _____
   _____

3. relaxing/concert
   _____
   _____

4. bored/conversation
   _____
   _____

5. excited/good news
   _____
   _____

6. frightening/roller coaster ride
   _____
   _____

7. interesting/museum
   _____
   _____

8. boring/book
   _____
   _____

Use Words Creatively

1. If they don't already know, tell your classmates what you do for fun. Also explain why you do it and when you do it.
2. With another student, ask two people outside of class what they do for fun. You can ask friends or strangers. Take notes on their answers and share your results with the class.

LEARNING STRATEGY

Remembering New Material: Writing about things you've heard or discussed helps you remember the words you've learned.

3. Write a paragraph about what you do for fun. If possible, use words from this chapter. Add a drawing or photograph.

Word Game

PANTOMIME

LEARNING STRATEGY

Overcoming Limitations: Playing games helps you relax and learn new words quickly.

Divide into two teams. Have a player from Team A pantomime (act without talking) an activity people do for fun. If the members of Team A guess the activity, they win a point and it is Team B's turn. A player from Team B repeats what the first team did, but uses a different activity. The team with the most points at the end wins.

Recycle

Do at least one of the following activities in small groups. Combine words from this chapter with words from previous chapters.

1. Eating is an activity people sometimes do for fun. For example, people eat popcorn or cotton candy because it is fun. Think of at least five more food items or eating activities that are fun.
2. You are a travel editor for a local newspaper. Your paper is focusing on *Fun Places Around the World* in its next edition. Think of three places that are known for particular activities that people do for fun.
3. Think about the times when you've had fun learning. What were you doing and how did you learn? Share these experiences with member of your group.

   Optional: Write your answers to the Recycle activities.

Review

Review the new words in this chapter by matching pairs with similar meanings.

grown up	family members
season	mature
buddy	problems
picture	summer
worries	antique
scrapbook	photo
parents	quiet
peaceful	practice
old	friend
train for	album

Test Yourself

Mia, a college student, surveyed several other students about their hobbies. She recorded the results of one interview, but 10 words or phrases are missing. Complete the conversation by putting the words where they belong.

stay fit	belong to	spend time	peaceful	season
foreign	take my mind off	exciting	members	club

MIA: Excuse me, do you have time to answer a few questions?

STRANGER: Sure. I need to _____ my test tomorrow.
1
I've been studying all day.

MIA: Well, this won't take long. I'm asking people what they do for fun.
How about you? How do you _____ when you're
2
not studying?

STRANGER: In the summer I power walk. Now it's the rainy _____,
3
so I do yoga.

MIA: Where did you learn yoga?

STRANGER: I have friend who told me about it. I really like yoga because it's
_____ but you can still _____.
4 5
MIA: How often do you practice yoga?

STRANGER: Oh, at least three times a week. Now I _____ a
6
_____ where _____ learn
7 8
several kinds of yoga.

MIA: Is yoga difficult to learn?

STRANGER: You have to be strong and flexible, and you have to practice regularly.

I have made many friends through yoga, mostly _____
9
students. It's _____ because I'm going to teach
10
one of my new friends a western exercise as soon as the weather gets

warm: power-walking!

Look Back

What did you learn about activities for fun in this chapter?

_____

_____

_____

_____

_____

Look Ahead

What else do you want to learn about activities for fun? How will you do this?

_____

_____

_____

_____

Tools: Can Software Help You Learn?

TOOLS: CAN SOFTWARE HELP YOU LEARN?

Will computers replace teachers? Will they replace textbooks? What can you learn using a computer? In this chapter, you're going to talk and write about using computers to help you learn.

PART 1: WORDS IN CONTEXT

Take a Look

Look at these ads. They describe computer programs for learning languages.

InterActive English gives the student dozens of options and types of activities. It responds to user input, giving every student control of his/her own learning. Students receive immediate feedback on their responses. They can access grammar explanations instantly and they can repeat an activity as many times as necessary.

Japanese Magic teaches the basics of written and spoken Japanese through a combination of interactive lessons and drills. Want to know how to write a word? *Japanese Magic* draws the characters for you, stroke by stroke— and pronounces them, too. Want the English translation of a word? Just click the mouse!

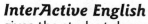

LEARNING STRATEGY

Remembering New Material: Learning new words in context helps you remember their meanings.

Read the descriptions again. Check the features that each product has, according to the descriptions you read.

	InterActive English	Japanese Magic
Allows the user a lot of choice	―――――	―――――
Gives the user a lot of control	―――――	―――――
Provides immediate feedback	―――――	―――――
Contains grammar explanations	―――――	―――――
Provides unlimited repetition	―――――	―――――
Draws characters	―――――	―――――
Pronounces words	―――――	―――――
Translates words	―――――	―――――

Threads

Learn to Speak Spanish **was one of the best-selling CD-ROMs in the United States in 1994.**

NewMedia magazine,
February 1995

Read About It

LEARNING STRATEGY

Overcoming Limitations: Pretending you know the meanings of new words helps you read more fluently.

Read the following newspaper article. Guess the meaning of any words you don't know.

Language software: The last word

by Jill Timothy

More and more people are learning to read and speak foreign languages from computers. They're using exciting new language programs that use color, sound, and motion. These new programs are much better than earlier ones that just replaced flashcards in drill-and-practice language learning.

Computers are useful in language teaching because they can display pictures, speak words aloud, and record speakers as they imitate the program's perfect pronunciation. Most foreign language training programs speak words aloud while displaying the word or phrase and a related picture. They repeat the word as often as the user clicks the mouse; they also move forward or back in the program, translate on demand, and never criticize you!.

Most people are interested in programs that teach Spanish, French, Japanese, English as a Second Language, Russian, German, Italian, and Chinese. For more unusual languages, teachers can buy special "blank" programs, called authoring systems, and create their own teaching programs. Dr. James Milton, head of the Midwest Language Institute, says the 700 language teachers in his program are creating computer-assisted language teaching courses for a variety of languages, from Arabic to Tagalog.

Check Your Understanding

With a partner, answer these questions about the article you just read.

1. Why are many people choosing computer programs to learn languages?
2. What are some languages you can learn using a computer program?
3. What should you get if you are a language teacher, and you want to make your own teaching program?
4. What are some of the advantages of learning a language with a computer program, according to the article?

LEARNING STRATEGY

Personalizing: Giving your own opinion on a topic makes the material more meaningful to you.

Threads

PLATO, the first computer language for creating instructional programs, was developed by Control Data Corp. in the early 1970s.

5. Fill in the following chart. State the advantages and disadvantages, in your opinion, of using a computer to learn a foreign language.

COMPUTER-ASSISTED LANGUAGE LEARNING

Advantages	Disadvantages

Word Bank

Here are the new words for this chapter. Add them to your Word Journal.

COMPUTERS AND LEARNING

option	authoring system
on demand	flashcards
drill-and-practice	computer-assisted
interactive	to imitate
software	to click
to have control (of/over)	to display
input	program
to respond	user
characters	feedback
mouse	to access
repetition	language teaching/learning
to criticize	

LEARNING STRATEGY

**Forming Concepts: Answering questions about new words—
analyzing them—helps you understand them better.**

Questions

1. What can you click when you want to make a computer do something?
2. What two-word adjective means *with help from a computer?*
3. How would you complete this sentence: *A good computer-assisted language learning program will display* _____ *on the screen.*
4. Find the two-word nouns in the Word Bank. How do the meanings of the parts help you understand the meaning of the whole words?
5. Does the *-s* ending in the following words sound like [s] or [z]: *flashcards, characters?*

Answers

1. *a mouse*
2. *computer-assisted*
3. *Display* means *pictures, a translation, a sentence, the correct answer:* anything that you can see on the screen.
4. *feedback:* information returned (*back*) to you; *flashcards:* cards you show quickly (in a *flash*).
5. Both *-s* endings sound like [z].

Synonyms

Thinking of synonyms for new words extends your vocabulary. Some words in the Word Bank have a lot of useful synonyms.

Work with a partner. Study the words in the following list. Then study the words in the Word Wheels. Match the words in the list to the words in the wheels that have similar meanings. Then add synonyms of your own. Look at the example before you start.

show	demonstrate	reply
tell	answer	mimic
copy	say	reproduce

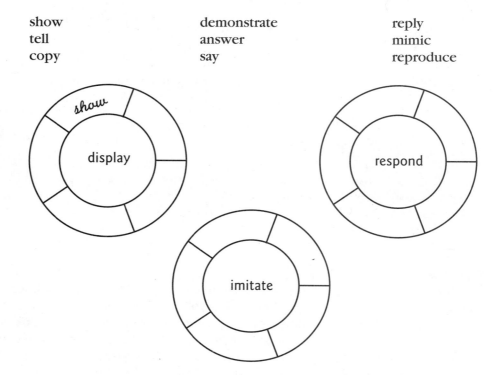

Word Forms: Nouns to Verbs; Verbs to Nouns

Some of the words in the Word Bank are nouns that have corresponding verb forms, or verbs that have corresponding noun forms.

EXAMPLE You can use a computer *program* to learn a language (noun); you can also *program* a computer to do a variety of things (verb).

Program (noun) and *to program* (verb) have the same spelling. Some of the noun/verb pairs have different endings.

EXAMPLE A good computer *responds* (verb) quickly when the user clicks the mouse; the user can see the *response* (noun) on the screen.

To respond is the verb form of the noun *response*. Notice the spelling differences between the two forms.

Work with a partner. Fill in the chart with the correct forms of the nouns and verbs in the following list. If a word has a star (*), that means there are spelling differences between the two forms.

display	user*
program	interaction*
input	click
criticize*	repetition*
respond*	imitate*

VERBS	NOUNS
_____	_____
_____	_____
_____	_____
_____	_____
_____	_____
_____	_____
_____	_____
_____	_____

Structure: Making Comparisons

When you talk about different ways of learning something, you can use comparison language. For example, you can say:

It's {
easier
better
faster
harder
more difficult
less fun
} to learn a foreign language with a computer program.

Most one-syllable adjectives end in *-er* when you use them in comparisons; you use *more* or *less* with most two- and three-syllable adjectives. Here's a list of common adjectives of both types:

ADJECTIVES WITH *-er* ENDINGS:		ADJECTIVES WITH *more* OR *less*	
*good ⟶	better	difficult ⟶	more/less difficult
easy ⟶	easier	impossible ⟶	more/less impossible
hard ⟶	harder	**fun ⟶	more/less fun
fast ⟶	faster	**slow ⟶	more/less slowly

Good has an irregular comparison form.
**Fun* and *slow* are exceptions to the one-syllable rule.

Also, when you make comparisons in talking or writing, you are discussing two (or more) things. You include both in the sentence with the structure:

BE + comparison adjective + *than.*

EXAMPLE Let's say you are comparing learning a foreign language by yourself and learning a foreign language in a classroom:

Learning a foreign language by yourself *is harder than* learning it in a class.

In small groups, use these words and structures to compare the following phrases.

BE + {
better
more/less difficult
easier
more/less fun
harder
more/less slowly
faster
more/less impossible
} than

1. learning a language in the classroom/on your own

_____

_____

_____

2. learning a language with a textbook/with a software program

_____

_____

_____

3. learning a language in your home country/in the country where it's spoken

_____

_____

_____

4. writing by hand/writing with a computer

_____

_____

_____

5. learning Language X [fill in]/learning Language Y [fill in]

_____

_____

_____

Use Words Creatively

LEARNING STRATEGY

Managing Your Learning: Sharing information with others gives you more opportunities for learning.

1. In small groups, talk about computers:
   • What are their uses? (Talk about uses today, and possible uses in the future.)
   • Do they make our lives easier or more difficult?
   Have a recorder write down your ideas and share them with the class.
2. Compare learning something on a computer with learning it in a classroom with a teacher.
3. In small groups, talk about different ways of learning a foreign language. Use comparison language, if you wish. In your discussion, think about the following:
   • computer-assisted language learning
   • independent study
   • video language-learning programs
   • classes
   • tutoring
4. Write a paragraph about 1, 2, or 3 above. Trade paragraphs with a partner. Read your partner's paragraph and tell him or her one thing you liked about it.

LEARNING STRATEGY

Forming Concepts: Playing with words helps you understand them better.

Threads

Computers can do many things at a dizzying speed. What they can't do is write papers, create ideas, read textbooks, or attend classes.

Dave Ellis in *Becoming a Master Student*

Word Game

PICTIONARY™

For this game, you need several 3 by 5 inch cards, some white drawing paper, some soft pencils (Number 1 or 2) to draw with, and a three-minute timer. Here's how you play:

Form two teams. Write several words from the Word Bank on 3 by 5 inch cards. Place each team's cards face down on a table. Flip a coin to see which team goes first.

One member of the first team—the person who's *IT*—picks an upside down card from the other team's pile. (He or she doesn't show it to the rest of the team.) Start the timer. The person who's IT then draws a picture representing the word or expression on the card.

    EXAMPLE   Word on card: mouse

The team members try to guess the word as he or she draws. If they guess before the time is up, they get a point. Then the other team has a turn.

Recycle

1. You are an educational psychologist. You're very excited about educational software because it makes learning easy for different kinds of learners. Explain to a group of students how educational software is useful for different kinds of intelligence.
2. You write about software for a computer magazine. Give your opinion of some software programs that teach and entertain at the same time.
3. You're a famous cooking instructor—you have a popular cooking show on TV. You want to create an interactive computer program based on your show to teach people to make your favorite recipes. Design the program with your group. What will it teach? How will the user interact with it? What additional information will it contain?

   Optional: Write your answers to the Recycle activities.

PART 4: ASSESSMENT

Review

Work with a partner. Review the meanings of words from this chapter by taking the following review quiz together:

1. Who is most likely to use an authoring system?
   a. a teacher
   b. a student
   c. a travel agent
2. Which of the following are good things about language teaching programs?
   a. They give you feedback.
   b. They criticize you.
   c. They are boring.
3. What do you call a person who is using a computer program?
   a. a mouse
   b. a character
   c. a user
4. If a computer program has a lot of options, that means it has a lot of
   a. choices.
   b. repetition.
   c. characters.
5. Which would be an old fashioned kind of language-teaching program?
   a. An interactive program
   b. A program that has video
   c. A drill-and-practice program

Test Yourself

Test your knowledge of the meanings of the words in this chapter by taking the following quiz. Read the letter. In it, a student describes a recent language-learning experience. Then fill in the blanks with the words from the following list:

feedback
drill-and-practice
imitate
displays
option
program
characters
software
flashcards
interactive

Dear Dad,

Since you're so interested in technology, I thought you might like to hear about the new _____ in the learning lab at school. It's a
1
computer _____ for learning Japanese. Since I want to
2
learn a little before my trip, I signed up for it.

I really like it. It has sound and color, and it's much more _____
3
than that boring _____ program we used to have. It
4
_____ your answers on the screen and gives you
5
immediate _____ so you always know when you've given
6
the right answer.

It's realistic, too. You hear a native speaker pronounce the words, and
_____ him. There's a recording _____,
7   8
so you can compare your pronunciation with his.

You can also learn Japanese _____. There's an
9
interesting game that helps you remember them. It's a lot better to learn them
with a game than the _____ we used to use.
10
Well, I'm going to the lab, now. See you next week!

Love,

Jennifer

Threads

A popular educational CD-ROM title can sell up to 9,000 copies a month.

PC Data, October–March, 1994

Look Back

What did you learn about computer programs for language-learning?

_____

_____

_____

_____

Look Ahead

What else do you want to learn about computer programs for language learning?

_____

_____

_____

_____

Tools: How Do You Get Information?

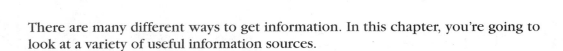

TOOLS: HOW DO YOU GET INFORMATION?

There are many different ways to get information. In this chapter, you're going to look at a variety of useful information sources.

PART 1: WORDS IN CONTEXT

Take a Look

Take a look at these photos of information sources. In small groups, identify each source and the kind of information you can get from it. Then, talk about if you've used each one and when and where you've used it.

a. _____

_____

_____

b. _____

_____

_____

c. _____

_____

_____

d. _____

_____

_____

e. _____
_____
_____

f. _____
_____
_____

Threads

Some synonyms for
"book" that you'll find
in a thesaurus: reference
work, edition, volume,
primer, treatise, work.

Microsoft 5.1 Thesaurus

Read About It

Libraries have just about every information source that exists. Read this excerpt
from a pamphlet that introduces the campus library to new students:

> Welcome to the Jones Memorial Library. There's a wealth of information on
> every subject at Jones. And you'll find a lot more than just books here. At first
> it may seem confusing, so we've written this QuickStart Guide to get you on
> the right track. Just look at the column on the left for the type of information
> you need. Then follow the arrows to the source on the right. The guide will
> also tell you where in the library you'll find the information source.

QUICKSTART GUIDE

If you need . . . →	Look for it in . . . →	Located in/on . . .
A phone number or address for a person or a business	A telephone directory	The Periodicals Room, on the 4th Floor—includes local, national, and international phone directories.
To find a book	The card catalog. Books are alphabetized by author, title or subject. You can also do a computer search with the on-line catalog	The Main Collection, on the 2nd Floor—includes both the card catalog and the on-line catalog for circulating and noncirculating books.
To locate a magazine or newspaper article	The *Reader's Guide to Periodical Literature*, InfoTrak (an on-line magazine source), or the *New York Times* Index.	The Periodicals Room, on the 4th Floor—most newspapers are on microfilm, also in the Periodicals Room.
To look up the meaning of a word	A dictionary	The Reference Room, on the 3rd Floor—offers several excellent abridged and unabridged dictionaries.
To find a synonym for a word	A thesaurus	The Reference Room, on the 3rd Floor—has several comprehensive thesauruses.
Basic information, facts, or statistics on almost any subject	An encyclopedia	The Reference Room, on the 3rd Floor—offers three current encyclopedias.

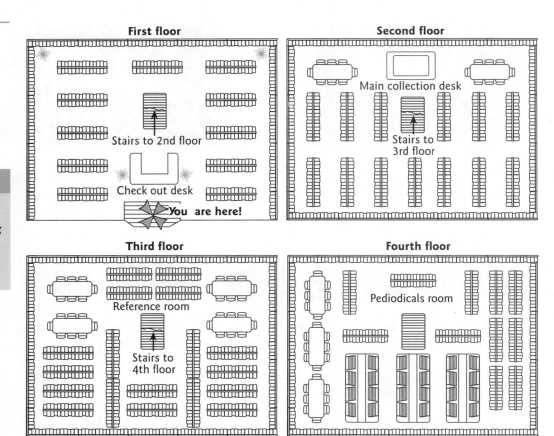

Check Your Understanding

Work with a partner and complete the following chart. Base your answers on information in the library pamphlet. Use the words and expressions in the following list:

a thesaurus	an encyclopedia
The Readers' Guide to Periodical Literature	a dictionary
the Madrid phone book	the on-line catalog
the Periodicals Room	the Reference Room
the Main Collection	the 2nd Floor
the 4th Floor	the 3rd Floor

IF YOU NEED . . .	LOOK FOR IT IN . . . (SOURCE)	LOCATED IN . . . (ROOM), ON . . . (FLOOR)
a magazine article about the 1996 Summer Olympics	_____	_____
another word for *progress*	_____	_____
the definition of *microfilm*	_____	_____
the phone number of the U.S. Embassy in Madrid, Spain	_____	_____
the year that the North Pole was discovered	_____	_____
the author of a book called *Baseball in April*	_____	_____

Word Bank

Here are the new words for this chapter. Add them to your Word Journal.

RESOURCE TOOLS

(tele)phone directory	noncirculating	to do a search
encyclopedia	dictionary	facts
(card) catalog	on-line	guide
to locate	a search	index
information	statistics	definition
synonym	to look up	comprehensive
abridged	microfilm	main collection
alphabetized	unabridged	circulating
reference room	to be located in/on	a wealth of
1st/2nd/3rd floor	periodical	

Questions

❶ Which words in the Word Bank are adjectives? Nouns? Verbs? Group the words in the list by part of speech. Put a star (*) next to words that can have more than one part of speech.

❷ Where is the stress in the following words: *encyclopedia, alphabetized, thesaurus?*

❸ Which word rhymes with *guide: wood   wide   weed?*

LEARNING STRATEGY

Forming Concepts: Focusing on how new words are used in a sentence helps you use them correctly.

❹ Which of these follows *located in?* Which follows *located on?*
the Reading Room   the 4th Floor

❺ How many syllables does *reference* have?

Answers

❺ *Reference* has three syllables, but in fast speech, it's hard to hear the second one.

❹ located in *the Reading Room;* located on *the 4th Floor*

❸ *Guide* rhymes with *wide.*

❷ encycloPEdia, ALphabetized, theSAUrus

❶ **Adjectives:** *reference,* * *periodical,* * *alphabetized,* * *on-line,* * *abridged,* * *unabridged,* * *circulating,* * *comprehensive.*
Nouns: *phone, directory, dictionary, thesaurus, encyclopedia, reference,* * *reference room, periodical,* * *(card) catalog,* * *a search, statistics, facts, information, guide,* * *synonym, microfilm, index,* * *definition,* * *1st, 2nd, 3rd floor, main circulation.*
Verbs: *to search (for), to locate, to look up, guide,* * *index,* * *alphabetized* *

Word Associations

You can stretch your vocabulary if you think about all the additional words associated with a single word. Word associations also help you remember word meanings. Here's how you do it. Just take a cue word, for example **periodical,** and say or write all the words it makes you think of: magazine, journal, *People,* review, newspaper, issue, publication, etc.

Now try this with the following words from the Word Bank. Use these guidelines to make associations. Think of words that are:

- similar to the cue word in meaning or form
- examples of the cue word
- in the same category as the cue word

directory: _____

reference: _____

catalog: _____

statistics: _____

information: _____

guide: _____

index: _____

LEARNING STRATEGY

Overcoming Limitations: Thinking of words you already know that are related to new words can expand your vocabulary.

Word Forms: Verbs to Nouns

Many of the verbs in the Word Bank have similar or identical noun forms. Being familiar with all forms of a word helps increase your vocabulary. See how familiar you are with the noun forms of these verbs from the Word Bank. Match the verb on the left to its correct noun form on the right.

Verbs	**Nouns**
to locate	an alphabet
to alphabetize	information
to index	a search
to catalog	a location
to guide	an index
to inform	a catalog
to search	a guide

Now, read the following sentences. Say whether the underlined words are verbs or nouns.

1. The librarian did a computer <u>search</u> to <u>locate</u> the <u>information</u> I asked for.
2. All the books in the library are <u>alphabetized</u> in the card <u>catalog</u>.
3. This <u>guide</u> <u>informs</u> you of the <u>location</u> of all the <u>reference</u> sources in the library.
4. It's your job to <u>locate</u> and <u>index</u> all of the art you'll need for your presentation.

Structure: Passive Forms

We sometimes use the passive voice when we talk about information sources.

EXAMPLE   The dictionaries *are located* in the Reference Room.

The passive voice is formed by BE + the past participle of the verb. You use it when the person or thing causing the action is not important. Look at these examples of verbs from the Word Bank:

Active Form	**Passive Form**
to locate	is/are located
to alphabetize	is/are alphabetized
to index	is/are indexed
to catalog	is/are cataloged
to guide	is/are guided
to inform	is/are informed

LEARNING STRATEGY

Forming Concepts: Learning grammar rules related to new words helps you understand both the meanings of new words and how they're used.

Complete these sentences with the passive form of the verb in parentheses.

1. (index) All the newspapers from 1965 to 1995 _____ in The Reader's Guide.

2. (alphabetize) Books _____ by author, title, and subject in the card catalog.

3. (locate) The phone books _____ in the Periodicals Room.

4. (catalog) All books in the library _____ in the on-line directory.

5. (guide) With InfoTrak, users _____ through an easy-to-follow periodical search program.

Use Words Creatively

1. In small groups, talk about your school or campus library:
   - Where is it? What hours is it open?
   - What can you find there?
   - Is it easy to use? Why or why not?
   - Do you use it often? Why or why not?
   - Which is your favorite room? Why?
   - Is it missing any important information sources? What?
   - What's one thing you would like to add to your library?

2. In small groups, compare two or more information sources. You can compare the card catalog with the computer catalog; one kind of encyclopedia with another; the encyclopedia with original sources (e.g., books, articles). Talk about:
   - how easy it is to use
   - how easy it is to find
   - the quality of the information

3. In small groups, think of and discuss any reference sources that have not been mentioned in this chapter.

4. Pick one of the following research tasks. Go to a library to get the information. Then report to the class on your experience. What reference source(s) did you use? How easy or difficult was it to get the information?

   Research Tasks
   a. Find the names of three women inventors and what they invented.
   b. Find the name and phone number of a Spanish-language bookstore in Los Angeles, California.
   c. Find three facts about refined sugar.
   d. Find out the birth date of the American author, Amy Tan.
   e. Find the author, publishing company, and publication date of a book titled *Baseball in April*.
   f. Find out the natural resources of Costa Rica.
   g. Find out where the saguaro cactus grows.
   h. Make up your own research task.

Word Game

FICTIONARY

Overcoming Limitations: Playing games with words gives you confidence to try new things.

For this game, you need two very good dictionaries. Here's how you play:

Form teams of four or five people. Flip a coin to see which team goes first. Pick a team captain. The team captain of the first team picks an unusual word from the dictionary. All the team members read the dictionary entry for that word. One team member writes down a correct definition of the word; the rest of the team members make up definitions that sound possible, but are incorrect.

EXAMPLE   Word: pingo

Real Definition: A small hill in an Arctic region, created by water pressure.

Sample *Fictionary* Definition: The Eskimo word for a baby penguin.

Take turns reading your definitions to the other team. The other team members try to guess—as a group—which definition is correct. If they guess correctly, they get a point. Then they have a turn.

Recycle

Do the following activity in small groups. Combine words from this chapter with words from previous chapters.

One group member is an information specialist. The others are doing research on various subjects. The researchers pick a topic and ask a specfic question about it. The information specialist tells them where or how they can find the information.

Topic	Question
places in a particular community	_____
famous women	_____
long-distance transportation	_____
food from different countries	_____
food ingredients	_____
travel abroad	_____

EXAMPLE   places in a particular community

Question: What's the address of the main post office in San Francisco?

Information Specialist: Look in the San Francisco phone book.

Review

Review the words in the Word Bank by performing the following role-play:

Work in pairs. One of you is the librarian, the other is a student who needs help. The student asks for help finding information and the librarian tells the student where he or she can find it in the library. Then trade places. Use the following information and the library guide on page 107 to begin, and then make up your own.

Information to Find
a phone number in New York City
the address of a school in Paris
a synonym for *difficult*
a book about the California Gold Rush
a magazine article on Kevin Costner
a definition of the word *eponymous*
population statistics for Brazil
a newspaper article about earthquakes

Sources
card catalog
on-line catalog
The Reader's Guide to Periodical Literature
a telephone directory
a dictionary
a thesaurus
The New York Times Index
an encyclopedia
the periodicals room
the reference room
the main collection

Threads

The printing press was invented by John Gutenberg in the mid-15th century.

Test Yourself

Test your knowledge of some of the words from the Word Bank by filling in the blanks in the following excerpt from a library guide. Use these words:

reference	locate
collection	circulating
floor	index
located	search
encyclopedias	catalog

Welcome to the Danforth Library. You'll find _____ books
on the 1st Floor, in the Main _____ . Both the card catalog and
the computer _____ are _____ in this department.
_____ materials, such as dictionaries, _____ and
other directories are in the Reference Room, on the 2nd _____ .
Librarians will help you _____ whatever information you need in
this department.

On the 3rd Floor, you'll find the Periodicals Room. The Periodicals Room
has The *New York Times* _____ and the *Reader's Guide to
Periodical Literature,* plus computer catalogs, such as InfoTrak. Reference
librarians will be happy to help with your _____ .

Look Back

What did you learn about words that describe different kinds of information
sources?

_____

_____

_____

_____

_____

Look Ahead

What else do you want to learn about different kinds of information sources? How
do you plan to do this?

_____

_____

_____

_____

_____

Threads

**Information becomes
knowledge when it's
actionable.**

Peter Senge.

Answers to
Selected Exercises

Check Your Understanding   p. 5

1. Answers will vary. Sample answers: Places Where You Buy Things—Coffee Shop, Supermarket, Drug Store; Places Where You Visit People—Hospital, Condominiums, Business Buildings; Places Where You Look at Things—Library, Museum, Park; Places Where You Borrow Things—Library, Bank; Places Where You Go for Help—Hospital, Drug Store, Police, Post Office.

2. school—learn new words
   hospital—visit a sick patient
   playground—have a picnic
   supermarket—buy groceries
   post office—buy stamps
   shopping mall—buy a shirt
   library—read a magazine
   restaurant—eat a meal
   museum—look at paintings
   theatre—watch a movie

3. school—teacher
   hospital—doctor
   playground—recreation supervisor
   supermarket—cashier
   post office—clerk
   shopping mall—store manager
   library—librarian
   restaurant—waitress
   museum—guide
   theater—usher

Adjectives   p. 8

1. spacious; new; popular; well-equipped; well-organized; modern

Review   p. 10

1. hospital
2. restaurant
3. above
4. supermarket
5. guide
6. playground
7. house
8. school
9. supermarket
10. library

Test Yourself   p. 11

1. community
2. apartment
3. school
4. restaurant
5. supermarket
6. post office
7. hospital
8. library
9. shopping mall
10. museum

CHAPTER 2 PLACES: HOW DO YOU GET THERE?

Check Your Understanding   p. 16

1. Four: airplane, car, train, ship
2. Answers will vary. Sample answer: Los Angeles
3. Answers will vary. Sample answer: Mexico City
4. Student Travel, Inc.; Travel Supermarket
5. Travel Supermarket
6. weekend rates
7. Sample answers: You don't have to pay for the miles you drive; you can drive as far as you want for one price.
8. Five: Puerto Vallarta, Ixtapa, Acapulco, Mazatlan, and Cabo San Lucas

Synonyms   p. 17

cheap—inexpensive
depart—leave
return—come back
itinerary—a travel plan
domestic—within the country
international—outside the country
fare—price
charter—to reserve for a group

Structure: Gerund Subjects   p. 18

1. Answers will vary. Sample answers: (a) Traveling by air (b) Traveling by sea
   (c) Traveling by train (d) Traveling by car . . .traveling by air
   (e) Traveling by train . . . traveling by car

Word Game   p. 19

Word Search

Review   p. 20

1. **c.** itinerary
2. **b.** one way
3. **c.** international
4. **a.** railpass
5. **c.** travel by train
6. **c.** both a and b
7. **c.** charter
8. **b.** coach
9. **a.** sea
10. **c.** mileage

Test Yourself   p. 21

1. prices/fares
2. destinations
3. international
4. Discount
5. Round Trip
6. first
7. cruise
8. Charter
9. mileage
10. prices/fares

CHAPTER 3 PEOPLE: WHO ARE THESE FAMOUS WOMEN?

Check Your Understanding   p. 27

1. Answers will vary.
2. Rosa Parks, Rigoberta Menchu, Golda Meir, Eleanor Roosevelt, Indira Ghandi, Benazir Bhutto
3. Answers will vary. Sample answers: Golda Meir, Amelia Earhart, Jackie Joyner Kersee, Indira Ghandi, Benazir Bhutto
4. Eleanor Roosevelt, Indira Ghandi, Benazir Bhutto
5. Ella Fitzgerald
6. Rosa Parks, Ella Fitzgerald, Eleanor Roosevelt, Amelia Earhart, Jackie Joyner Kersee, Maya Angelou
7. Answers will vary. Sample answers: All of them.
8. Answers will vary. Sample answers: All of them.
9. Answers will vary.
10. Answers will vary.

Synonyms   p. 30

talented—skillful
start—begin
solo—alone
brave—courageous
speak out for—represent
shy—timid
fight—struggle
dedicated—committed
accomplishment—achievement
smart—intelligent

Antonyms   p. 31

afraid—courageous
death—birth
lose—win
dead—alive
unknown—famous
end—initiate
stupid—intelligent
follow—lead
destroy—create

Word Forms: Verbs to Nouns   p. 31

exploration, creation, education, inspiration, initiation, performance, establishment, improvement

Review   p. 34

1. courageous—afraid
2. famous—unknown
3. talented—skillful
4. strong—weak
5. smart—intelligent
6. alive—dead
7. win—lose
8. native—indigenous
9. brave—courageous
10. start—initiate
11. lead—follow
12. solo—alone

Test Yourself   p. 34

1. famous
2. inspires
3. improve people's lives
4. skillful
5. talented
6. face difficulties
7. struggle
8. accomplishments
9. courage
10. dedication

Check Your Understanding — p. 41

Answers will vary. Sample answers:

1. f.	11. g.
2. b.	12. b.
3. g.	13. a.
4. e.	14. b.
5. d.	15. e.
6. f.	16. d.
7. g.	17. e.
8. c.	18. c.
9. b.	19. a.
10. a	20. f.

Prefixes — p. 43

1. Answers will vary.
2. Both begin with *inter*-; *international* means among nations; *interpersonal* means among (or between) people.
3. Answers will vary.
4. *Interpersonal* means among or between people; *intrapersonal* means within oneself.
5. The diagram on the left shows deductive thinking; the one on the right shows inductive thinking.

Word Forms: Nouns, Verbs, Adjectives — p. 44

Nouns	Verbs	Adjectives
reflection	reflect	reflective
rhythm	X	rhythmic
sense	sense	sensitive
verb	verbalize	verbal
X	visualize	visual
solution	solve	X
music	X	musical
distinction	distinguish	distinctive
intelligence	X	intelligent

Review   p. 48

Class Activities	Type of Intelligence	Why?
1. Students draw a picture of what they have read	*Visual/Spatial*	*Relies on students' ability to visualize*
2. Students talk to each other about a story they're reading	*Verbal/Linguistic*	*Students use language*
3. Students analyze similarities and differences of grammar ruless	*Logical/Mathematical*	*Students analyze patterns*
4. Students perform a skit	*Body/Kinesthetic*	*Involves movement*
5. Students use colored markers to highlight words they want to learn	*Visual/Spatial*	*Emphasizes visual memory*
6. Students learn a song to practice a grammar structure	*Musical/Rhythmic*	*Uses song and rhythm to assist in learning*
7. Students write a story in teams	*Interpersonal*	*Involves communication in groups*
8. Students give an oral presentation of their backgrounds and goals	*Intrapersonal*	*Requires reflection about self*
9. Students write poems with new words that rhyme	*Musical/Rhythmic*	*Rewards students who do well with sound patterns*

Test Yourself   p. 49

1. Verbal/linguistic
2. Logical/mathematical
3. recognize
4. relationships
5. Visual/spatial
6. Body/kinesthetic
7. musical/rhythmic
8. patterns
9. interpersonal
10. intrapersonal

Check Your Understanding   p. 53

1. thick or thin crust
2. three
3. Swiss Sweet Factory
4. Le Bon Pain Sourdough French Bread Bakery
5. boiled, grilled, smoked
6. candy
7. Le Bon Pain Sourdough French Bread Bakery
8. Monterey Pasta Company; you get a discount if you buy a lot there.
9. La Salsa
10. Answers will vary. Sample answers: Sushi Maru, Monterey Pasta Company, The Italian Eatery.
11. Answers will vary.
12. Emperor's Garden
13. The Italian Eatery
14. Le Bon Pain Sourdough French Bread Bakery
15. Le Bon Pain Sourdough—French
    Monterey Pasta Company—Italian
    La Salsa—Mexican
    The Italian Eatery—Italian
    Chicago Hot Dogs—American
    The Sandwich Express—American
    Emperor's Garden—Chinese
    Swiss Sweet Factory—Swiss
    Sushi Maru—Japanese

Associated Meanings   p. 55

1. juicy
2. thin
3. available
4. counter
5. sugar-free
6. daily
7. favorite
8. marinated

Antonyms   p. 56

thin—thick; sweet—sour; cooked—raw; stale—fresh; dry—juicy; unavailable—available; high-cal—low-cal; vendor—buyer

Review p. 58

1. Vegetarian
2. take out
3. counter
4. daily
5. raw
6. eatery
7. meal
8. sweet
9. Sumptuous
10. sour

Test Yourself p. 59

1. favorite
2. varieties
3. gourmet
4. ethnic
5. sushi
6. daily specials
7. Chinese
8. kids' menu
9. low-cal combo
10. delicious

CHAPTER 6 FOOD: WHAT'S IN IT?

Check Your Understanding p. 64

1. Answers will vary. Sample answers: eggs, spaghetti sauce, bread; olive oil, honey, tomatoes
2. granola bars; artificial flavor, BHT
3. chickens raised without cages
4. vine-ripened tomatoes
5. flour with vitamins and minerals (niacin, iron, thiamin, riboflavin)
6. brown sugar; other sweeteners: honey, corn syrup
7. a preservative
8. the tomato is ripened on the vine, before it is picked.
9. Answers will vary. Sample answers: A hormone is a chemical that affects growth or milk production in an animal. Food you might find them in: milk, beef.

Word Forms   p. 66

to process—processed; to ripen on the vine—vine-ripened; to grow organically—
organically grown; to enrich—enriched; to sweeten—sweetened

1. Enriched
2. Processed
3. organically grown
4. sweetened
5. vine-ripened

Word Associations   p. 67

Answers will vary.

Review   p. 69

1. soybean
2. corn syrup
3. color
4. wheat flour
5. vine-ripened
6. riboflavin
7. BHT
8. pesticides
9. organically grown
10. enriched

Test Yourself   p. 70

1. Ingredients
2. Organically
3. oil
4. soybean
5. sugar
6. artificial
7. preservative
8. enriched
9. iron
10. nonfat

Check Your Understanding
p. 75

reason for going abroad—to study; where did she go—India; who did she stay with—volunteers in refugee camps, Indian families; what did she learn—about the political problems in Tibet; how did the experience change her life—she learned the Tibetan language and now helps Tibetan refugees

Word Forms: Nouns, Verbs, Adjectives, Adverbs
p. 77

Nouns: People	Nouns: Things or Fields	Verbs	Adjectives	Adverbs
adventurer	adventure	X	adventurous	X
server	service	serve	X	X
ecologist	ecology	X	ecological	ecologically
enrollee	enrollment	enroll	enrolled	X
ecotourist	ecotour	X	X	X

Word Forms: People Nouns and Thing Nouns
p. 78

1. volunteer—volunteerism; tourist—tourism; mountain biker—mountain biking; counselor—counseling; scuba diver—scuba diving; bird watcher—bird watching; kayaker—kayaking; intern—internship
2. a. internship
   b. Scuba diving
   c. bird watcher
   d. volunteer
   e. tourist
3. Answers will vary.

Infinitives of Purpose
p. 79

1. Margaret went to Croatia to volunteer with refugee programs.
2. For my next vacation, I'm going to Costa Rica to go birdwatching in the rainforest.
3. Ping went to San Francisco to enroll in ESL classes.
4. Adi went to France to learn French.
5. Ken is going to Sweden this summer to work on a farm.

Review   p. 81

tank—scuba diving
binoculars—bird watching
helmet—mountain biking
paddle—kayaking

   2. **b.** have different meanings
   3. **a.** mean about the same thing
   4. **a.** Helping repair roads
   5. **b.** Bird watching
   6. **a.** You don't get paid
   7. **c.** because they want a lot of practice speaking the local language.
   8. **b.** The country you were born in

Test Yourself   p. 82

   1. abroad
   2. study
   3. enrolling
   4. study program
   5. camp counselor
   6. ecotour
   7. exotic
   8. native
   9. scuba diving
  10. adventure

CHAPTER 8 FUN: WHAT DO YOU DO FOR FUN?

Check Your Understanding   p. 86

   1. Answers may vary. Sample answers: Alone: Wei, Aimée. With others: David, Christine, Scott, Dennis
   2. Answers will vary. Sample answers: David, Christine, Wei.
   3. Answers will vary. Sample answers:

      Christine—runs—stay fit/spend time with friends—every weekend
      Wei—reads—to improve English/to learn things—a couple times a week
      Scott—goes to stock car races—they're exciting/takes his mind off his worries—once a month in spring and summer
      Dennis—goes fishing—it's peaceful/fun—once a month

   4. Photographs, stamps, letters, antiques. Second answer will vary.

Review   p. 90

1. grown up—*mature*
2. season—*summer*
3. buddy—*friend*
4. picture—*photo*
5. worries—*problems*
6. scrapbook—*album*
7. parents—*family members*
8. peaceful—*quiet*
9. old—*antique*
10. train for—*practice*

Test Yourself   p. 90

1. take my mind off
2. spend time
3. season
4. peaceful
5. stay fit
6. belong to
7. club
8. members
9. foreign
10. exciting

CHAPTER 9 TOOLS: CAN SOFTWARE HELP YOU LEARN?

Check Your Understanding   p. 96

1. Answers will vary. Sample answers: The new programs are exciting; they're better than the old ones.
2. Spanish, French, Japanese, English as a Second Language, Russian, German, Italian, and Chinese.
3. An authoring system.
4. They can display words, speak words aloud, record users, display pictures, the user can move at his or her own pace, they translate, they don't criticize you, etc.
5. Answers will vary.

Synonyms   p. 98

display: show, demonstrate
respond: answer, tell, say, reply
imitate: copy, mimic, reproduce

Word Forms: Nouns to Verbs; Verbs to Nouns   p. 98

Verbs	Nouns
to display	(a) display
to program	(a) program
to input	input
to criticize	(a) critic
to respond	(a) response
to use	(a) user
to interact	interaction
to click	(a) click
to repeat	repetition
to imitate	imitation

Review   p. 102

1. **a.** *A teacher*
2. **c.** *are interactive*
3. **c.** *a user.*
4. **a.** *choices.*
5. **c.** *A drill and practice program*

Test Yourself   p. 103

1. software
2. program
3. interactive
4. drill-and-practice
5. displays
6. feedback
7. imitate
8. option
9. characters
10. flashcards

Check Your Understanding   p. 108

- magazine article about Summer Olympics—The Reader's Guide to Periodical Literature—the Periodicals Room, 4th floor
- another word for *progress*—thesaurus—the Reference Room, 3rd floor
- definition of microfilm—a dictionary—the Reference Room, 3rd floor
- phone number in Madrid, Spain—a telephone directory—the Periodicals Room, 4th floor
- year North Pole was discovered—an encyclopedia—the Reference Room, 3rd floor
- the author of *Baseball in April*—card catalog/on-line catalog—the Main Collection, 2nd floor

Word Forms   p. 110

to locate—a location
to alphabetize—an alphabet
to index—an index
to catalog—a catalog

to guide—a guide
to inform—information
to search—a search

1. search—noun, locate—verb, information—noun
2. alphabetized—verb, catalog—noun
3. guide—noun, informs—verb, location—noun, reference—noun
4. locate—verb, index—verb

Structure: Passive Forms   p. 111

1. are indexed
2. are alphabetized
3. are located

4. are cataloged
5. are guided

Review   p. 114

Answers will vary. Possible response:

Student: I need a phone number in Paris, France.

Librarian: Go check the telephone directory for Paris in the section with all the phone books.

Test Yourself   p. 114

1. circulating
2. collection
3. index
4. located
5. Reference

6. encyclopedias
7. floor
8. locate
9. catalog
10. search